Authority and Challenge:
Lectures on Ancient and Medieval Indian History

The K.M. Ashraf Memorial Lectures

Authority and Challenge: Lectures on Ancient and Medieval Indian History

Mohammad Habib
Irfan Habib
Kumkum Roy
Firdos Anwar

The History Society
Kirori Mal College
University of Delhi, Delhi

Authority and Challenge: Lectures on Ancient and Medieval Indian History

First Published, 2014
Reprinted, 2026

ISBN 978-93-5002-278-8

Published by
AAKAR BOOKS
28 E Pocket IV, Mayur Vihar Phase I
Delhi 110 091 India
www.aakarbooks.com

Typeset at
Arpit Printographers, Delhi

Printed at
D.K. Fine Art Press, Delhi

Contents

Preface

The History Society, Kirori Mal College, University of Delhi is pleased to present before you the K.M. Ashraf Memorial Lecture, 2013 delivered by Prof. Irfan Habib and also two other papers presented by Dr. Firdos Anwar and Prof. Kumkum Roy during the seminar on 'Authority and Challenge: Processes of State and Social Formation in India' which followed the K.M. Ashraf Memorial Lecture, 2013.

The K.M. Ashraf Memorial Lecture, as far as the records suggest was started in 1966 and the first lecture was delivered by the eminent historian Prof. Mohammad Habib. However the memorial lecture in the honour of K.M. Ashraf could not be sustained and was discontinued most probably in its early years. After a long gap of nearly four decades it was revived by the History Society, Kirori Mal College in 2012, on a very modest scale where the emphasis was more on recalling his days at Kirori Mal College in which his students such as Prof. Harbans Mukhia, Prof. Arjun Dev, and Mr. Zahoor Siddiqui participated.

In 2013, at the request of the Society, Prof. Irfan Habib agreed to deliver the K.M. Ashraf Memorial Lecture which was on 'Questionings within Religious Thought: The Experience of Islam' . He also gave us the permission to publish the same. A senior member of the Society, Dr. Firdos Anwar had a copy of the first K.M. Ashraf Memorial Lecture delivered by Prof. Mohammad Habib. The lecture was on the theme, 'Some Aspects of the Foundation of the Delhi Sultanate', which he provided for publication in this volume.

The Society is extremely grateful to the Indian Council

of Historical Research for providing us a generous grant to organize the memorial lecture and seminar. We would also like to express our gratitude to Prof. Irfan Habib, Prof. Kumkum Roy and Dr. Firdos Anwar for providing their memorial lectures and seminar papers to the society. Prof. Kumkum Roy's and Dr. Firdos Anwar's papers were titled 'Making Laws, Breaking Laws: Brahmanical and Buddhist Perspectives from Early India' and 'Leading Family Groups of the Mughal Mansabdars under Shah Jahan' respectively.

1

Some Aspects of the Foundation of the Delhi Sultanate[1]

Mohammad Habib

Mr. President, Workers of the Ashraf Memorial Fund, Ladies and Gentlemen, I wish I could express in words my gratitude to you for organizing these lectures in memory of my deceased ex-pupil and friend, the late Dr. Kunwar Muhammad Ashraf and of giving me the great privilege of delivering the first lecture. I hope one of the lectures that follows will give a biography of Dr. Ashraf. Here I am concerned in working out, with reference to the Delhi Sultanate, the principles that inspired Ashraf as a historian and as a citizen. Neither as a student nor at any later stage did I find the slightest touch of communalism in Ashraf. He believed in searching for the truth and in expressing his opinions without hesitation, and nothing was further from his thoughts than a theological interpretation of the history of any country; though in a scientific assessment of the historical phenomena, the theological element cannot be ignored, for theology—unlike religion—is the fetter that holds back social progress. From this point of view, the history of India is not the history of the Hindus, Muslims, Jains, Parsis, Sikhs or Christians. It is simply the history of Man in India, and Man in India has never been cut off from the rest of the world. As Alberuni observed about 1030 A.D., "If a science or an idea has conquered the whole world, every nation appropriates a part of it; so called the Hindus."[2]

The Problems—I cannot begin my discussion of the Delhi Sultanate better than by repeating a question that my friend, Professor Parmatma Saran, has posed in his contribution to the quest for Empire.[3] How did the Ghorian kingdom with its 12,000 horsemen[4] succeed in overthrowing Rajput kingdoms whose resources were several times greater? The question can be pushed further. How did it happen that the government established at Delhi by a small number of foreign Turks, whose communication from their homeland had been cut off forever was recognized as the only possible centre for the administrative unity of India with a Muslim king at the top from Qutbuddin Aibek to the revolution of 1857?

It was an odd position which will never recur and it can be explained on the understanding that the history of India during this period is not to be explained in theological terms—that is in the terms of the Shariat, the Shastras or the Smritis. For the pure theologian for whom the world has always been, and must be, a perpetual war of creeds, such a situation seems impossible. Still the evidences for the existence of the Delhi Sultanate, the great provincial dynasties of the fifteenth century and the Mughal Empire are too obvious to be ignored. Respect for Delhi, whatever be the complexion of the government, has somehow gone into our blood. It was the alternative to Calcutta for the so-called mutineers of 1857.

To find a correct answer to the two questions asked above, we must critically examine both the international situation as well as the social system of India at the time of the Ghorian invasion.

The International Situation—The international situation, which Indian historians generally ignore, has to be briefly described. The Caliph of Baghdad was supposed to be the head of the Muslim world. But his opposition was precarious. Baghdad for a long time had been a mere city-state, and the Caliphs usually were mere figureheads. Of the 28 minor Abbasid Caliphs, eight were killed, two were blinded, and three were deposed but probably not killed and one was asked to abdicate. One of the blinded Caliphs, Al Qahir Billah, lived for years after his deposition and used to beg with other blind men in the Juma mosque of Baghdad.[5] From the frontiers of Baghdad to the river Oxus lay the extensive domain of the empire or Sultanate of Khwarasm (1157-1218). It was the greatest monarchy among the Muslims and was believed to have some 4,50,000 trained soldiers in his service.[6] Trans-oxiana or the land between the Oxus and the Jaxartes along with Turkestan (modern Sinkiang) was governed by the Ghor Khans, a non-Muslim dynasty of Chinese origin. The author of the Tabaqat-i-Nasiri gives them a good certificate for equity and justice. The Ghor Khans governed Trans-oxiana through tributary Muslim princes, and by an old treaty, which they considered onerous; the Khwarasm Shahs also paid tribute to the Ghor Khans and were entitled to their assistance. The reigning Ghor Khan was a woman, but what mattered to the Muslim world her remarkable general, Taniku Taraz. Far off, now about 28, he was learning these principles of military and administrative organization, which were to make him the most feared conqueror in world history.

It will be easier to understand what happened if we ignore details and fasten our attention on the main facts. In 1192 Muizzuddin Ghori defeated Prithvi Raj at the second battle of Tarain. The Ghorian conquest of northern India, the character of which we will have to examine later, took about fourteen years, for in 1205-06 we find that Ikhtiyaruddin Khalji, after establishing himself at Lakhnauti, was venturing on an invasion of Tibet.

In 1205-06, both Ikhtiyaruddin Khalji and Muizzuddin

Ghori came to grief. The former was driven back from Tibet and almost his entire army perished in his attempt to swim across a river, which may have been a branch of the Brahmaputra. Unable to face the curses of the relatives of the soldiers whom he had led to their doom, he took to his bed and died or was assassinated soon after. "Some misfortune must have overtaken my master, Muizzuddin", he said before dying. His guess was correct. In order to put a final end to his protracted quarrel with Alauddin Khwarasm Shah, Muizzuddin decided to march from Ghor to Khwarasm near the north of the Oxus. It was a foolhardy enterprise and Muizzuddin had to suffer from the consequences. The local inhabitants declared a *jihad* or holy war against the Ghorian invader and their ruler appealed to Ghor Khan for help. Taniku Taraz, rightly calculating that Muizzuddin would have no alternative but to retreat, marched not towards Khwarasm but Andkhud to cut off Muizzuddin's return journey. Some Ghorian officers fled before Muizzuddin was surrounded by the Ghor Khani troops on a summer afternoon. The battle that followed the next day could only have one end. Muizzuddin fought courageously, but when only about a hundred men were left with him, one of his slaves wisely took hold of his bridle and led him to the safety of the fort of Andkhud. Through the intermediation of a Ghor Khani Muslim chief, the Sultan Salatin of Samarkand, Taniku Taraz allowed Muizzuddin to return to Ghor on condition of surrendering everything he had. Muizzuddin talked wildly about preparing to attack the Ghor Khan after three years, but the battle of Andkhud put an end to the Ghorian Empire everywhere except in India.

After Shahabuddin's assassination in 1206, his slave Tajuddin Yilduz established himself at Ghazni and declared his independence. But Firoz Koh, the family seat of the Ghorian dynasty, went to the heirs of Ghiyasuddin Ghori, who acknowledged Khwarasm Shah as their overlord. In 1212 or 1213 Khwarasm Shah decided to give the region we now call Afghanistan as a jagir to his eldest son, Jalaluddin Mankbarni. Malik Ziauddin surrendered Firoz Koh and spent the rest of his life at Khwarasm. Yilduz was driven to India, where he was defeated and killed by Iltutmish. Thus some seven years after Muizzuddin's death, the Ghorian state completely vanished from the scene. But the worst was still to come.

The Mongol Conquest of Muslim Asia—In 1216, some twelve years after the death of Muizuddin Ghori, Chengiz Khan, who had already plundered the whole of China north of the yellow river, marched from Mongolia to the Jaxartes, a journey of some three months, with an army of over ninety thousand disciplined warriors, the cruellest and the bravest the world has yet seen. The objective was clear. He wanted to establish the rule of his dynasty over the whole of Muslim Asia and so much of the Christian world beyond as the Mongol horse could reach.[7] For this purpose the mere liquidation of Muslim ruling dynasties, subordinate or overlord, was not enough. Chengiz was sure that the Mongol government over Muslim Asia could not be established without his perpetrating the massacres such as the world had never seen. The stupid policy of Alauddin Khwarasm Shah, who instead of challenging him on the eastern bank of the Jaxartes, divided his enormous army of four or five lakhs into small contingents which he put into the arks (inner citadel) of his cities while to save his own life he fled eastwards to die on an island of Caspian, made Chengiz Khan's task very much easier. The open island was left to him and he could easily crush such resistance as individual cities and forts could offer.

Chengiz Khan followed three different policies with regard to three different regions.

Turkestan—The Muslim and non-Muslim princes and cities of Turkestan (Sinkiang) were already accustomed to a non-Muslim overlord. The chief princes of the region had already gone to Qara-quram and offered their allegiance to Chengiz. From this region, therefore, Chengiz demanded nothing more than food supplies for this passing troop.

Trans-Oxiana—The region between the Oxus and the Jaxartes, dominated by the great cities of Samarkand and Bokhara, had gradually become a centre of Islamic culture since its conquest by the Arabs some five centuries earlier. Cities east of the Jaxartes belonged culturally to Transoxiana rather than to Turkestan. Chengiz had Samarkand and Bokhara levelled with the ground while the wealth of the citizens, whether above the ground or below it, was seized. Concerning other cities, if they surrendered without fighting as most of them did, the soldiers in the ark were put to the sword while the inhabitants were brought out of the city so that the Mongols could plunder their houses. This plunder, we are told, took place only once. All young men were captured and added to the Mongol army as hashr for the immense non-military work that the army needed; roughly ten muslims belonging to the hashr were put under one Mongol soldier. Chengiz had four sons to provide for, and as he had decided to give Turkestan and Trans-oxiana to his second son, Chaghtai, he decided to leave Chaghtai some citizens and peasants, who would be able to pay taxes. To his second son, Juji, Chengiz gave Khwarasm and the whole of the western steppe up to Southern Russia and

Juji's descendant, known as the *Ulus-i-Juji* or the golden horde reigned there till they were overthrown by Timur. Tului, the youngest and cruellest of Chengiz's sons, was by law entitled to the hereditary principality of Mongolia. Chengiz had decided that his third son, Ogatai, would succeed him as Khan. But to ensure the power of Chengiz and successors it was necessary that wholesale massacres should leave no capacity for resistance in the subject population. "Wherever there was a king or a ruler or the governor of a city that offered him resistance," Juwayni tells us, "Chengiz annihilated him together with his family and followers, kinsmen and strangers; so that where there had been a hundred thousand people, there remained, without exaggeration, not a hundred people alive."[8]

Khwarasm, Merv, Khorasan, Herat, Naishapur, Afghanistan—This statement is borne out by the destruction of the greatest medieval cities of Ajam, which we can now survey. The inhabitants of Khwarasm, the capital of the empire, fought the Mongols in every street and lane but when the city was captured, they were all taken out. Children and women were reduced to slavery; about a hundred thousand skilled craftsmen, whose services the Mongol needed, were sent to the regions of the east. Every Mongol soldier was required to execute twenty-four inhabitants and no one was left alive. At Merv, the capital of the former Seljuk empire, Tului brought all the inhabitants out of the city and ordered them to be put to death. Every Mongol had to execute three to four hundred prisoners. But one, Sayyid Izzuddin Massaba, and a few others, managed to save themselves by hiding and after the departure of Tului, they spent thirteen days and nights in counting the corpses they could easily find. The total came to one million and three hundred thousand. Naishapur, the capital of Khorasan, had submitted; nevertheless an excuse for attaching it was found. The dead were counted for twelve days and there were one million and forty thousand corpses, not including the corpses of women and children.[9] At Sabzwar, not far from Naishapur, the Mongols had already killed and counted 70,000 corpses. At Herat, Tului put to death 12,000 soldiers who were in the service of Jalaluddin Mankbarani, placed a Mongol Shuhna in charge of the city and returned to join his father at Taliqan. But Chengiz was not satisfied. He sent one of his generals, Ilchikdi Hoyan, with instructions to put the whole population of Herat to the sword. Ilchikdi after a siege of six months and seventeen days overpowered the city and martyred a little less than one million and six hundred thousand of the inhabitants.

After destroying Samarkand and Bokhara, Chengiz proceeded against Tirmiz on the northern bank of the Oxus. The inhabitants refused to submit; the city was overpowered and all the inhabitants were massacred. Balkh, south of the Oxus, was a prosperous city and had 50,000 notable inhabitants. When Chengiz crossed to the southern bank of the Oxus, the city offered its submission. Nevertheless all the inhabitants were taken out of the city on the pretext of being counted and put to death. Jalaluddin Mankbarni, the eldest son of Alauddin Khwarasm Shah, who had the misfortune of having an Indian mother and a dark skin, succeeded in reaching the region of Ghor and Ghaznin, which his father had assigned to him after a series of narrow escapes. He won a victory at Parwan but was unable to make any permanent resistance and fled across the Indus before Chengiz's eyes. The inhabitants of Bamian, Taliqan, Ghaznin and other cities in Afghanistan, were slaughtered ruthlessly, not even the garrisons on the highest hill-forts could escape the Mongols.

The shoulder-blades of sheep, which Chengiz consulted as omens, would not permit him to cross the Indus in order to march through Northern India to China. However, his task had been accomplished. Two of his generals, the brothers Yeme and Subatai, had marched with an army of thirty thousand across Northern Persia and after marching back through the Quipchaq steppe north of the Caspian. The kingdom, or rather Imamat of Alamut with its 105 forts in Persia and Iraq had offered its humble submission to Chengiz, and so had the rulers south of the Persian desert. The territory of the Caliph was, for the time, left untouched. All territories not assigned by Chengiz to his sons were put in charge of governors, who continued the work of plunder, slaughter and Chengiz could, therefore, return leisurely to Mongolia where he died in 1227.

Ogatai Qa-an (1227-41) is pictured by Ata Malik Juwayni as a kindly soul. He was always tipsy and this gave the impression of being kind-hearted. Nevertheless the policy of Chengiz was followed with one modification. Now that the Mongols had no rivals left, it was realized that the policy of wholesale massacres had been overdone. If the inhabitants of the cities and the rural areas were totally annihilated, there would be no trade and no crops and consequently no revenues for the state. The chief expansion of the Mongol empire was in Europe; Ogatai gave all possible assistance to his cousin, Batu, son of Juji, and the Mongols reached as far as Dresden. An end was put to the Kin kingdom in China, the last ruler of which burnt himself to death. In India, the Mongols captured Lahore, but the day after they had done so, news arrived that the great Qa-an, ruler of the east and the west, had died during a fit of drunkenness. Tului had died of the same complaint a little earlier and Chaghtai died soon after.

According to the yasa of Chengiz Khan, when a Qa-an died, his successor was to be elected by a Quriltai or assembly of princes and high officers from among the descendants of Chengiz. But till a Quriltai had decided the matter, the senior widow the deceased Qa-an was to administer the affairs of the centre, Chengiz Khan could annihilate all rivals; but no precepts or yasa he left could prevent his descendants from fighting with each other after all non-Mongols had been completely crushed. Tarakina Khatun, Ogatai's senior widow, acted as regent till 1246; then her son, Kayuk, was elected by a Quriltai to which Batu, the greatest of the Mongol princes had refused to come. A battle between Kayak and Batu was only prevented by the timely death of the former. At an informal Quriltani in 1248 Batu got Mangu Khan, the eldest son of Tului, elected as Qa-an, and this was confirmed by a formal Quriltai in 1251. Manu planned that one of his brothers, Qublai, should complete the conquest of China and establish his dynasty (the Yuen dynasty) there. It lasted till 1370. Halaku, the youngest son of Tului, was assigned India up to the Ravi along with Persia and commissioned to put an end to the the kingdom of Alamut and the Caliphate of Baghdad. The Ilkhani dynasty founded by him lasted till the death of Sultan Abu Said Khan in 1334. In the same year Amir Timur, whose massacres were second only to those of Chengiz Khan, was born. The descendants of Chaghtai and Ogatai joined to maintain an independent power in Turkestan and Trans-oxiana. The central authority of the Mongolian empire vanished with the death of Mangu Qa-an in 1260, but the four states or dynasties into which it broke up—the golden horde or *Ulus-i-Juji* of southern Russia, the Khans of Persia, the Chaghtai-Ogatai empire of Central Asia and the Yuen dynasty of China—lasted well into the fourteenth century.

It was necessary to give some details of the total collapse of Muslim political, economic and social life in Muslim Asia to put the growth of the empire of Delhi in its proper perspective.

Indian trade relations with Arabia, in particular with Yaman and the Persian Gulf region, had existed for centuries before the rise of Islam. So far as Muslim Arabs were concerned, we find from the Tuhfatul Mahajirin[10] and other early records that the Hindu rajas gave to the Muslim merchants land in the suburbs of the great towns, where they could have their houses, mosque, storeroom and grave yards. Some of these settlements, like Badaun, became centres of Muslim culture and learning. The Arab travellers in the country have left us a fair quantity of literature. Judged by Al Beruni's standards, it leaves much to be desired but the Arabs must have succeeded in acquainting the Hindus with the two chief features of Muslim social life—absence of caste and complete equality in religious matters.

Monarchy among the Muslims—What was the political condition of India when Chengiz retreated from the Indus in 1222? There may have been forty to fifty thousand Turks, Khiljis and other foreigners in the country led by three rivals—Iltutmish, Qubacha and Khalji maliks of Lakhnauti. They could not return home, for the Mongols would have killed them. India had become their homeland and they could expect no help from abroad. Competing with them, though not necessarily opposed to them, were, plenty of Ris, Ranas and Rawats with their forts and armies. For centuries the Brahmans had taught them that they had allied genealogies. Nevertheless, during these same centuries all Indian rulers had been fighting with each other, and the bitterness engendered had been so great that they had been unable to make a joint stand against Muizzuddin Ghori; and his officers had succeeded in capturing the larger towns and the main trade routes. Northern India had not known a unified administration since the time of Harsha. Today there are no Turks in India; they were absorbed in our population. But it is an unidentifiable fact that in the thirteenth century, they held all important government posts and had succeeded in giving administrative unity to northern India, which though shaky and incomplete was something on which the future could be built.

So far as courage and self-sacrifice are concerned, the advantage lay wholly with the Rajputs. The Turks may have had better strategy and tactics, but they never came upto the Rajput standard of valour.

I am inclined to attribute the success of the Turks in India to three facts, which historians of the thirteenth century have generally ignored. They had, far away from India, developed a type of monarchy, which though immoral and hideous, had one great advantage. If the monarch was an able man, it gave him complete control of the government, including the appointment and dismissal of all officers, and of the natural resources of the state. Secondly, they were accustomed to large-scale administration, for which this type of monarchy had been planned. Thirdly, so far as was compatible with the principles of hereditary monarchy, they preferred merit to birth. For example, the names of the fathers of Qutbuddin Aibek, Iltutmish and Balban have yet to be discovered. The first two principles mentioned above justify a digression because they go back to the early generations of Islam.

The apparatus of a state or an executive government with a central authority maintaining peace and order was unknown to Arabia till the rise of Islam. It would not be correct to say that the Prophet Muhammad established a government for Arabia, for he did nothing of the sort. He had no police force, no office, no paid clerks, no personal servants and no locked room or treasury; his army consisted of volunteers and most of its expenses were met by subscriptions. Before his death he had made a series of treaties with the clans and tribes of Arabia by which he was obliged to maintain peace and order while the tribes and clans paid a specified contribution to the expenses of the centre.[11] The Quran repeatedly orders the Muslim to obey Allah and His Prophet, but it also directs the Prophet 'to consult the Muslims about their affairs'. The Prophet in his thatched mosque was always available to the Muslims. But subject to the criticism and suggestions from his own followers, he had the initiative in all matters. It is the claim of Sunni Muslims that the Four Pious Caliphs (632-61) who followed him, also lived a simple life and decided matters by consultation and advice.

Some matters of great importance can only be referred to here in passing. The Prophet, according to the Sunnis, appointed no successor, thereby leaving the whole organization of public affairs to the opinion of the Faithful (*ijma-i ummat*). The first Caliph, Abu Bakr (632-34), was elected at a tumultuous meeting, which Muslim good sense refused to regard as a precedent. The second Caliph, Umar (634-44), was nominated by Abu Bakr. The third Caliph, Usman (644-56), was elected by a committee of six which

Umar appointed after his assassination. The fourth Caliph, Ali (656-61), was publicly elected but not exclusively by the inhabitants of Medina; also among the voters was a group of persons who had been responsible for the murder of the third Caliph. The Pious Caliphate does not, unfortunately, provide us with a principle for devolution of the supreme command of the state. It is unfortunate also that as the Four Pious Caliphs appointed no guards for their personal protection, three of them were assassinated. Amir Muawiya (661-80) who followed Ali, converted the Caliphate, while retaining its name, into a monarchy, or rather an empire, by the simple process of appointing his son, Yazid, as his successor and taking the oath of allegiance to him from all his high officers. But the Ummayyad monarchy that grew out of this process, enjoyed all the power that had been exercised by the Prophet and the Pious Caliphs (without the criticism and advice which had restrained them), the most important being the appointment and dismissal of all government officers and the appropriation of the revenues of the state as the private property of the king.[12]

What is known as the Saracenic or Arabian conquest of the outer world came in two floods—the first during the reign of Umar and the first six years of the reign of Usman (634-50) and the second during the reign of the Umayyad Caliph, Walid bin Abdul Malik (705-15). The frontiers of the Muslim population today are curiously enough where Walid left the frontiers of his Caliphate in 715 A.D. Now for about a century and a half after the death of the Prophet it was generally believed that all Muslims must of necessity live under one authority, and the Umayyad Caliphate had to arrange for an administrative machine that could govern the Muslim world from Southern Spain to the Frontiers of China. Though this conviction gradually disappeared, we find a series of mammoth empires in Muslim Asia following in the wake of the Umayyads (661-750)—the Great Abbasids (750-861), the Ghaznavids (999-1040), the Seljuqs (1137-57) and the Khwarasmians (1157-1220).

Social Classes in India—Returning to the small number of Turks left in India after 1222, it should not be difficult to understand that when circumstances forced them to the decision that India was their only home, they would also visualize it as one land with one capital and one government. The first conflict of which we read is between Iltutmish and Qubacha and of Iltutmish and the Khalji maliks. Iltutmish was successful against both. But the basic question was their relation with the sons of the soil— their Hindu neighbours.

Bernier observed in the reign of Aurangzeb that the Mughal government was reluctant to interfere with Hindu customs and this is true of the Delhi Sultanate also. Hindu laws show no trace of Muslim influence and the main changes have appeared in them after the establishment of Indian freedom (1948). Muslim law and custom, on the other hand, have been deeply influenced by Hindu concepts, under the Shariat principle known as 'Urf'.

Still the Muslim settlement in India—it is not fair to call it a conquest—could not but have some definite effect on the social system of India. Indian society has from very early times been divided into two exclusive groups—the four Aryan castes, who are in different degrees heirs to Aryan culture and the Chandalas or non-caste groups, whom the British called 'Scheduled Castes' and to whom Gandhiji gave the title of Harijans. The latter are still with us, roughly equal in number to the Muslims in the Indian

Union. Our Constitution, which declares 'untouchability' to be an offence strives to give them the same status and opportunities as to other citizens. But we all know how much remains to be done. It will be more convenient to discuss this unfortunate class first.

The famous Code of Manu, which may have been written as late as the third century A.D., gives the high-water mark of the rigidities of the caste system. It classes as Dasyus all those tribes which are not born from the mouth, arms, thighs and feet of the Brahman, whether they speak the language of the *mlechchhas* (barbarians) or of the Aryans. The former are the Greeks, Persians and Turks; they need not trouble us for they could look after themselves. The primary victim of the caste system was the Indian non-caste or the Chandala. "The dwellings of the Chandalas and Schwapachas," says the great Code, "shall be outside the village; they shall be Apaputras, and their wealth shall be dogs and donkeys. Their dress shall be garments of the dead, they shall eat their food from broken dishes, black iron (shall be) their ornament and they shall always wander from place to place. A man who fulfils a religious duty shall not seek intercourse with them; their transaction (shall be) among themselves, and their marriages with their equals. Their food shall be given to them by others (than an Aryan giver) in a broken dish; at night they shall not walk about in villages and towns. By day they may go about for the purpose of their work, distinguished by marks of the king's command, and they shall carry corpses (of persons) who have no relatives, that is a settled rule. Dying without the expectation of a reward for the sake of Brahmans and of cows, or in the defence of women and children, secures the beatitude of those excluded (from the Aryan community, Vahya)."[13]

No Persian or Arabic account describing the condition of the non-caste groups, defined exactly by the Code of Manu as "persons excluded from the Vahya or Aryan community," during the Ghorian period has yet been found. But less than two centuries earlier Alberuni left an account of them. Substantially he does not differ from Manu, but he surveys them from the view-point of their production and profession; he could only describe what he saw in a part of India and his list of the non-caste guilds is incomplete.

"The castes from the very beginning," Alberuni writes, "have only been four.... Between the latter two castes (the Vaishya and the Sudra) there is no very great distance. Much, however, as these classes differ from each other, they live together in the same towns and villages, mixed together in the same houses and lodgings."

"After the Sudra follow the people called Antyaja, who render various kinds of services, and who are not reckoned among any caste, but only as members of a certain craft or profession. There are eight classes of them, who freely marry each other, except the fuller, shoe-maker and weaver, for no others would condescend to have anything to do with them. These eight guilds are (1) the fuller, (2) the shoe-maker, (3) the juggler, (4) the basket and shield-maker, (5) the sailor, (6) the fisherman, (7) the hunter of wild animals and of birds, (8) and the weaver. The four castes do not live together with them in one and the same place. The guilds live near the villages and towns of the four castes, but outside them.

"The people called Hudi, Doma (Domba), Chandala and Bhadatau are not reckoned among any caste or guild.

They are occupied with dirty work, like the cleansing of villages and other services. They are considered as one sole class and distinguished only by their occupations. In fact they are considered like illegitimate children; for according to general opinion they descend from a Sudra father and a Brahmani mother as the children of fornication; therefore they are degraded outcastes...."

"Of the classes beneath the castes, the Hadi are the best spoken of, because they keep themselves free from everything unclean. Next follow the Doma, who play on the lute and sing. The still lower classes practise as a trade killing and infliction of judicial punishments. The worst of all are the Bhadatau, who not only devour the flesh of dead animals but even of dogs and other beasts."[14]

Alberuni's list of guilds is obviously incomplete. He tells us nothing of stone-workers, metal workers, masons, etc. The guilds were local organizations and not all-India institutions and neither Alberuni nor anyone else could have compiled a complete list of all the non-caste guilds of India. He also gives us no information about the agricultural groups, who then, as now, may have belonged to both caste and non-caste groups. Finally since his information was directly confined to the Punjab, he tells us nothing about the non-Aryan tribal groups that have survived from his time to ours.

Now so far as the Turkish settlement in India is concerned, some postulates may be safely laid down. No Muslim thinker has been haunted by that horror at "the mixture of castes," which we find in the Code of Manu. Illegitimacy among the Muslims may involve a social stigma and a denial of the rights of inheritance, but according to the basic concepts of Islam the illegitimate are as much entitled to salvation as the legitimate. Lastly the Muslims of those days, unlike their Hindu contemporaries, did not believe in the doctrine of *chhut* or irremovable physical contamination; there is nothing so dirty that water cannot clean it or, failing that, the breeze and the sun.

The easy march of the Ghorian Turks through northern India proves that the non-caste groups did not support the local rulers against them; a stiff opposition by the working groups of India would have certainly halted the march. Further, the ease with which the cities of north India fell before the armies of Qutbuddin Aibek seems to show that the assertion that the non-caste working groups were compelled to live outside the city walls is not without foundation. A city without the normal quota of workers, from the sweepers to the armament-makers, would be absolutely helpless before a besieging army, and we do not find a single city in the Trans-Gangetic plain offering a stout-hearted resistance. The Turks had no idea of reforming the Hindu social system, but their own outlook on the matter led them to give relief to the non-caste groups in two ways— first, the non-caste groups were allowed to live within the cities and given the normal rights of city-dwellers such as the right of owning and selling lands and houses and getting water from the wells and tanks of the city. Secondly, they were enrolled as wage-earners for such work as they could do, including service in the army. When Alauddin Khalji marched from Karra to Delhi during the rainy season of 1296 and enrolled some 60,000 men, both Lashkari and non-Lashkari, he made no inquiries about anybody's caste. On the question of 'untouchability' the precept of Sunni Islam is clear: The mouths of all men are clean, regardless of their religion, and the mouths of all animals are clean, except the dog and the pig.

Conversions to Islam—It remains to inquire about the thorny question of conversions to Islam. We have extensive data concerning the conversion of early Muslims by the Prophet. But conversions to Islam outside Arabia—in Northern Africa, Syria, Iraq, Persia, Central Asia, etc.—is a puzzling question. The Christians have carefully recorded the labours of their early missionaries; the Muslims have no missionary labours to record. There have been many so-called religious movements among the Muslims, but they have either been of a sectarian character, like the great Ismaili movement, which for centuries challenged the orthodox, or they have, like the mystics, sought to make existing Muslims into better Muslims. We find no trace of any missionary movements for converting non-Muslims. Medieval Islam was converting creed, but it failed to develop any missionary activity for three definite reasons. First, in most newly conquered countries the Muslims established themselves as a governing class and they were not inclined to increase their number. The non-Muslims were not invited into the creed, but they thrust themselves into it and the governing class had no means of preventing this.

Secondly, the growth of Islamic culture could not possibly keep pace with the very rapid expansion of the Caliphate. In what are the majority Muslim areas today, Muslim culture grew in the course of centuries. The third difficulty lay in the character of the religion itself. Islam is a city-creed in so far as it postulates a community or Jamaal. The Quran itself makes a distinction between the city-dwellers and the 'Arab or the bedouins of the desert; the latter are directed to call themselves Muslims but not Mumins (true believers) for the true faith has not yet gone into their hearts. We have to remember that most of Muslim Asia is steppe-land interspersed with oases and great cities, and it was in these great cities that Muslim culture flourished. It was very difficult for Muslim culture and devotion to religious rites to permeate the social life of the wandering dwellers of the steppes. Babur, for example, quotes a letter from his uncle, Mahmud Khan, a Mongol chief, to a renowned mystic complaining that his tribesmen, though formally inducted into Islam, were still following their old Mongolian ways of life.

So far as our country is concerned we have to confess frankly that no trace of a missionary movement for the conversion of non-Muslims has yet been discovered.[15] To be very frank about it, by the time the Turks came to India, the great thinkers of Islam had lost all faith in conversion. Their attitude is best expressed by two verses of Maulana Jalaluddin Rumi: "To every people God has granted a level of moral culture (Sirat): also to every people He has granted a religious technique (is te lah). The religious technique of the Muslims is best for the Muslims, the religious technique of the Hindus is best for the Hindus."

But the complete silence of written records does not mean that we do not know of the two great things that happened. In what may be called the backward tracts of our country—Sind, West Punjab, East Bengal and Kashmir— Islam for various reasons, equally unconnected with forcible conversion or freedom of religious choice, succeeded in making itself the religion of the majority. Kashmir, to start with, was far from being a backward tract. Alberuni declared that "Kashmir and Banaras were the two high schools of Hindu culture." But the southern passes to India were closed by the Kashmir rulers. and cut off from its homeland, Hindu culture degenerated to such an extent that Harsha-deva (1089-1101) could without any fear of opposition not only plunder the temples but go out of his way and have the divine images insulted by naked mendicants. But when Harsh-deva proceeded to plunder the landlords or dhammaras, they rose against him and killed him.[16] In 1320 the country was invaded by the Mongols who indulged in arson, rape and murder throughout the Valley. The kings and the Brahmans fled but among the inhabitants who remained the caste system completely disappeared. Muslim ways of life were gradually adopted by the people as the only possible alternative, for their only connection then was with Northern Afghanistan and Central Asia.

There was nothing to attract the higher Hindu classes to Islam in the heart of India from the river Ravi to the Brahmaputra, where Hinduism was a vital creed. A good part of this region comprised the home provinces of the Delhi Sultanate and the Mughal Empire, but there was no necessary contradiction between the two. The non-caste guilds, which were excluded from the Aryan community, may be divided into two classes guilds whose work was unclean or entailed the sin of *jiv* or *jeev hatya* (killing of living creatures) like the fishermen and the butchers, and guilds whose work was essentially clean, like those of the fuller and the weaver, but who for some historic reason found themselves among the lowest of the non-caste groups. Since many of these guilds or *biradaries* had adopted Islam by the end of the thirteenth century, and our histories are silent about the matter, we have no alternative but to assume that conversions to Islam were the result of group decisions. The guild of weavers at some places may decide to join the new creed, while at other places they may decide to adhere to their old religion. Shaikh Nasiruddin Chiragh tells us that in his youth he went to pray among the mango-groves in the neighbourhood of Ayodhya, and when he gave the call for the afternoon prayer, the weavers left their looms and came to pray with him. He also says that in his youth the different working-class groups had different graveyards in Delhi, but with the growth of Muslim consciousness, the differences in graveyards disappeared. These conversions only took place in the cities and the small *qasbas* or townships. In the rural areas or the open countryside there seem to have been no conversions at all. Islam, from the social view-point, had little to contribute to the Indian countryside; it does not recognize the Indian seasons and has no seasonal festivals; its mythology, borrowed from pre-Muslim Persia, was too alien to make any impression on the Indian peasant, who had absorbed the converted non-caste groups may have amounted to about 40 per cent of the total non-caste groups in the cities, and this section, though without any political consciousness, would all be in favour of the new regime.

This brings us to a curious contradiction in the economic position of the Islamic society in India. If you only study the political histories of India, such as Elliot and Dowson have translated into English, I will not blame you if you have the impression that the governing classes of medieval India were a body of trained exploiters, who worked hard but enjoyed all the great luxuries of life. But if you study the mystic records, such as the *Fawaidul fuwad* (Conversations of Shaikh Nizamuddin Aulia), the *Siyarul Aulia* (History of the Chishti Silsilah), the *Khairul Majalis* (conversations of Shaikh Nasiruddin Chiragh) you will be left with the impression that the mass of the Muslims belonged to the lower middle class or the upper working class. The teachers were poor and their pupils were poorer. For a time in Delhi Shaikh Nizamuddin Aulia and his mother were maintained by a working class woman, whose source of livelihood was grinding corn. Shaikh Nasiruddin Chiragh used to feel very happy when he found that his visitor had such a secure means of livelihood as cultivating a field or teaching boys in a mosque. So far as the mass of the Muslim community is concerned, the impression left by the mystic records is correct. The governing class was only a trifling fraction of the Muslim population; and the life of a government officer, as Shaikh Nizamuddin Aulia pointed out, was very precarious and unhappy. Most government officers fell into misfortunes sooner or later, either because they were punished for their misbehaviour or because the policy of the government changed. Shaikh Nasiruddin was asked to pray for a *malik*, who had been imprisoned and was thrashed every day. He refused to do anything about the matter. "Those who enter government service should be prepared for the consequences," he remarked. The misfortune of the Muslims of India throughout the ages has been due to the fact that they have never been able to get a footing in the production system of the country, except as artisans. The happiest groups during the Delhi Sultanate were the Hindu bankers (*sahas*), the transport merchants (*tujjar*) and market-merchants (*saudagar-i-bazari*). Next to them came the well-to-do *zamindars*, called Rais, Ranas and Rawats, whose security was guaranteed by the Delhi Sultanate so long as they paid their tribute and performed some specified services. There could be no Muslims among the *zamindars*.

Character of the Delhi Sultanate—I have to close this paper with a few remarks about the Delhi Sultanate, which must not be visualized like a modern state or even like the Mughal Empire. In its early stages it was a purely exploiting concern like the early East India Company. An impartial historian will be unable to give a better certificate to Muizzuddin Ghori, Aibek, Iltutmish and Balban than to Clive, Warren Hastings and Wellesley. But just as the British exploiters, without intending to do so, laid the foundation of an Indian middle class and helped our country to come up-to-date, the Turkish exploiters, without intending anything of the sort, helped the administrative unification of the country through their personal ambitions. Nevertheless governing India exclusively through Turkish slave-officers was a hopeless task. The successors of Iltutmish could not keep their hold over the Rajput forts he had conquered. Balban was so afraid of the Mongols that he never ventured to challenge a Hindu Rai, and all his energy was concentrated in crushing his Turkish rivals.

The real founder of the Delhi Sultanate was Alauddin Khalji, who brought considerable qualifications to his task. He had no book knowledge but plenty of experience and paid no attention to what the *ulema* said. He was a "non-practising Muslim": though he knew how to say his prays, he never attended the Friday congregation and never fasted. Since God had put him at the head of the state, he claimed that it was his duty to serve 'all the people of God'. "I do not know that will happen to me on the Day of judgment," he said, but fear of the unseen did not prevent him from shedding blood, when this was clearly demanded by the welfare of the country. Since the excellent work of my friend, Dr. Kishori Saran Lal, is available to all students, I need only refer in passing to those features of the great Sultan's work which have left an indelible mark on the history of our country. In the second or third year of his reign, Barni tells us, Alauddin put an end to the last remnant of the Turkish nobility. "Some were killed: others were imprisoned in distant forts; their families and followers were overthrown and their property, about a crore of *tankas*, was brought to the public treasury." Hereafter the Sultan could appoint whomever he liked without regard to race or creed. The great problem of the day, however, were the Mongols. Whoever succeeded in defeating them would succeed in governing India. The Mongols twice reached Delhi, but after a tremendous effort Alauddin succeeded in beating them back and his general, badr, succeeded in levying the *jizya*[17] on the inhabitants of Ghazni. Alauddin claimed suzerainty over the whole of Northern India and later on Southern India also. But he took under his direct administration only a small part of the country; the rest he left to the Rais, Ranas and Rawats, whose administration was better than anything he could give. If we keep this in mind, his Rajputana policy becomes clear. In case a Rai was defeated, the sultan tried to find a suitable prince from the defeated dynasty; if no suitable prince was available, he assigned the central government of the conquered territory to one of his officers, but the Rawats of the old regime were left to administer their lands, forts and armies. Under medieval conditions of communications and transport, no better type of unified state was possible. It is much to be regretted that his successors, in particular Mohammad bin Tughlaq, by putting too great a burden on the administrative machine caused a part of it to collapse.

The governing class organized by Alauddin lasted with

many changes till the death of Feroz Shah Tughlaq. More Hindus and converts from Hinduism were enrolled among the governing class by Mohammad bin Tughlaq and Firoz Shah. It is impossible to give a good certificate to any governing class, and the governing class of the Khaljis and the Tughlaqs could be no exception. To start with, Ziauddin Barani gives it an exception. To start with, Ziauddin Barani gives it an excellent certificate for efficiency but certainly not for character. But gradually, especially during the long reign of Firoz Shah the efficiency gradually vanished and was replaced by slackness and corruption. I will content myself by referring to two prize posts of the reign held by converts from Hinduism. Khan-i Jahan Maqbul, and Andhra whose Hindu name was Kannu (flower), was a good Wazir as Wazirs go; but he insisted on keeping two thousand slave-girls recruited from all countries from Byzantine to China and dressed them in fine robes. One has to assume that they were dressed at the cost of the tax-payer; also Firoz Shah settled an annual grant of eleven thousand *tankas* for every son of the Khan-i Jahan and of five thousand *tankas* for every daughter. Imadul Mulk Bushir Sultani had started his life as a slave of Rai Ranmal Bhatti and became Firoz Shah's minister of war. The annual gross revenue of Firoz Shah's empire was a little over six crores of *tankas*, but when Imadul Mulk died, his estate was estimated to be more than eleven crores—i.e. about two years' gross revenue of the whole empire.

We need not wonder that with so much corruption, and the oppression it must have entailed, the Delhi Sultanate vanished into thin air. Still we must not visualize it as having been a religious institution. This admission is frankly made by Ziauddin Barani, a great Muslim religious fanatic, in his *Fatawa-i Jahandari* (Advice XI) which he seems to have written in the seventh year of Firoz Shah's reign. "The desire for overthrowing infidels and knocking down polytheists," he says, "does not fill the hearts of the Muslim kings (of India). On the other hand, out of consideration for the fact that they are payers of tribute and protected persons (*zimmis*), these non-Muslims are honoured, distinguished, favoured and made eminent; the kings bestow drums, banners, ornaments, cloaks of brocade and caparisoned horses upon then and appoint them to governorships, high posts and offices. And in their Capital (Delhi), owing to the status of which the status of all other Muslim cities is raised, Muslim kings not only allow but are pleased with the fact that infidels build houses like palaces, wear clothes of brocade and ride Arab horses caparisoned with gold and silver ornaments. They are equipped with a hundred thousand sources of strength. They live in delights and comforts. They take Muslims into their service and make them run before their horses; the poor Muslims beg of them at their doors; and in the capital of Islam, owing the edifice of Islam is elevated, they are called Rais (great rulers), Ranas (minor rulers), Thakurs (warriors), Sahas (bankers), Mehtas (administrators) and Pandits (priests)."[18]

It is possible to ignore the tolerant policy of the state, which Barani has here reluctantly portrayed and condemn the regime owing to cases of religious persecution which (I frankly confess) are not difficult to find. Nevertheless, we do not find any anti-Muslim slant in Kabir Das and the great Hindu saints who came after him. They tried to find what was best in Islam and Hinduism and to reconcile the two. That is the problem before us also. We have to select all that is good in all the creeds as well as in modern science and build a prosperous and secular India on that basis with the light of morning in her eyes.

NOTES

1. This is a part of the Dr. K.M. Ashraf Memorial Lecture delivered by Prof. Mohammad Habib (Prof. Emeritus, Aligarh Muslim University, Aligarh) at Kirori Mal College, University of Delhi on October 26, 1966.
2. Sachau, *Alberuni's India,* Vol. I, p. 152.
3. *The History and Culture of the Indian People,* Vol. 3, Bharatiya Vidya Bhawan, Bombay.
4. *Cambridge History of India,* Vol. III, p. 30. The figure of 12,000 horsemen is probably correct.
5. *Rausatus Safa,* Vol. III, p. 173-174.
6. Juwayni's *Tarikh-I Jahan Gusha,* which devotes one volume each to Khwarasm Shah, the Mongols and the heretics of Alamut has been translated into English by Mr. Boyle. It is a UNESCO publication.
7. The earliest account of the Mongols is to be found in the last chapter of the *Tabqat-i-Nasiri,* which was written by Minhajus Siraj, the chief qazi and Sadr of Delhi, who was free to write as he liked. But he was about eighteen years at the time; he claims to have fought the Mongols and was one of the few persons who succeeded in escaping from them to India. What Minhaj tells us is reliable so far as the various parts of Afghanistan are concerned. But for distant regions, like Khwarasm, Minhaj relies upon rumours, which are definitely incorrect. The first reliable history of the Mongols which has survived is the *Tarikh-I Jahan Gusha* printed in Gibbs' memorial series written by Alauddin ata Malik Juwayni, a secretary of Halaku Khan. Since the Mongols did not wish to hide out but to publish an exact account of their massacres, Juwayni had no difficulty on that score. But he wrote in the intervals of business and there are gaps in his work. Rashiuddin, a minister of the Mongol rulers of Persia (called II Khans) tried to fill these gaps in his *Jamaiut Tawarikh,* of which only some parts have been published. Some regional histories, like the *Tarikh-I Hirat* also appeared, and they have been used by later works like *Tauzatus Safa.* The only Mongol work that has survived

in a Chinese translation is Yuan-chao-pi-shi (*Secret History of the Mongols*). It confines itself to Chengiz's career in Mongolia and has been translated into English by Dr. Wei-Kwai-Sun (published by the History Department of Aligarh Muslim University).

8. *Jahan Gusha*, Persian text, Vol. I, p. 17.
9. *Rauzatus Safa*, Vol. V, p. 37, Persian text (Newal Kishore).
10. The Arabic original has been lost. The Persian text, such as has survived, has been edited by Dr. M. Nainar (Madras University).
11. The original texts disappeared but Iba-i Sa'd (in the time of the Abbasids) succeeded in collecting several volumes of these treaties from living memory.
12. The Arabic for 'Kings' is malik, but it is only used for rulers of minor stature.
13. *The Code of Manu* (Buhler's translation), Chap. X, 51-55, 62.
14. Sachau, *Alberuni's India*, Vol. I, pp. 100-02.
15. Some cheap mystic books now current attribute conversions to Muslim mystics on the basis of the miracles they performed. So in order to believe in the conversions one has to believe in the miracles as well. But all such books will be found on examination to be later-day fabrications. Muslim mysticism, by its very nature, is "a postgraduate creed": it just could not be used for missionary purposes.
16. M.A. Stein's translation of *Kalhana's Rajtarangini,* Book VII (Verses IC87-1098).
17. In the Shariat textbooks, which have no relevance to actual facts, the jizya means "a poll-tax on a non-Muslim for remaining a non-Muslim." But in our records it means any tax which is not a land-tax. Thus Ziauddin Barani speaks of the jizya and khiraj being levied by the pre-Muslim emperors of Persia; he also complains that the Rais of his time collected from the Hindus, who belonged to their own creed, more khiraj and jizya than the kings of Delhi.

    In a curious sentence Shaikh Nizamuddin Aulia refers to the demand of a collector of land-tax from a Muslim mystic. "Either pay the jizya or show me a miracle," suzerainty from the Rais. At the marriage of Khizr Khan (February 2, 1312) he implies that the Rais and maliks assembled at the court had equal status.
18. Habib and Afser, *Political Theory of the Delhi Sultanate*, p. 48.

2

Questionings Within Religious Thought: The Experience of Islam

Irfan Habib

As we see religions now, they appear to be organized systems of belief and practice, with an emphasis on some form of afterlife. In general, they claim to derive their authority from what their followers hold to be texts or traditions of special sanctity or supernatural origins. Religions are further divisible into those which are non-theistic and those which contain as their centrepiece a belief in God. Zoroastrianism and the three Semitic religions (Judaism, Christianity and Islam), which belong to the second category, appear to have the same major features in their perception of the divine order: God, angels, Prophet, Judgement Day, and hell and heaven. In Islam, a very detailed legal code (*Sharī'at*) is also furnished, covering various aspects of life, on the basis of which punishments in this world and rewards and punishments in the next are envisaged for each human being.

Clearly, while religion may be a source of solace for the individual, it may yet be a diversion from the real source of oppression in material life.[1] Apart from this major external contradiction, religion itself cannot escape tensions within it, which must arise as it encounters divergent perceptions of ethics and social values, influences of other belief systems, and intrusions of reason, logic and science, which have a long past of their own. A large part of the history of any religion must consist of the questionings of its orthodox positions by ideas that derive from these various sources (which themselves are ever-changing). The following is a preliminary study of how such questionings arose in early Islam, and continued to be raised during its sojourn in

India. In this I draw particular inspiration from Dr. K.M. Ashraf's insistence on the need for a critical and close study of Islamic religious texts.[2] I cannot, however, claim anything beyond tentativeness for my present effort.

As is recognized in any standard work on Islamic history the conquest of Syria in 634, soon after the death of the Prophet, brought the Arabs into contact with Greek thought and science. From this originated the Mu′tazalite movement that sought to introduce some Hellenistic rationality into Muslim theology, as may be seen in its allowance for free will as against strict predestination, its insistence on the created nature of the Qurān, as against its being uncreated, and its assertion of the principle of justice governing God's action, as against His absolute freedom from any limitation.[3]

But the Mu′tazilites were, after all, theologians. There arose too in Islam, under the same Hellenistic influence, a succession of scientists who sometimes let their thoughts wander wherever reason took them. Muqaddasī, one of the great geographers of Islam, writing in 985, wondered whether it would not 'have been better if the vast sums of money spent on mosques had been spent on roads and caravanserais and frontier fortresses'.[4] This was rationality in its full splendour.

The same spirit of independence is shown by a great mathematician and scientist of the next generation, Abū Raihān Alberuni, the author of a seminal work, *Kitābu′l Hind* (c. 1035), on Indian civilization. Clearly unmindful of Muslim assertions of the corruption that Christian Gospels have allegedly suffered from, he unreservedly admires the ethics that the New Testament represents: "To offer to him who has beaten your cheek, the other cheek, also to bless your enemy and to pray for him: Upon my life, this is a noble philosophy." He does not seem to care that this is not what Muslim theology preaches.[5] He does not hide too his admiration for the *Bhagavad Gīta*, which he held to be the principal monotheistic text of Hinduism.[6] He is even able to quote with approval Vyāsa's dictum that once you have acquired the requisite knowledge of the elements— "adhere to whatever religion you like; your end will be salvation."[7] Knowledge is thus put on a higher pedestal than faith.

Though Alberuni did not know Greek or Syriac, he had been deeply influenced by Hellenistic works, translated into Arabic.[8] But there was another externally driven stream too, whose roots went to Iran. This ultimately created another and, in some ways, perhaps a more troublesome source of dissent for Islamic orthodoxy.

Iran had been subjected to a long and devastating conquest by the Arabs The wound to Iranian psyche is immortalized in words put in the mouth of an Iranian commander by Firdausī (c.1010), a contemporary of Alberuni and author of the Iranian national epic, the *Shāhnāma*:

> From mere drinkers of camel's milk and lizard-eaters,
> The Arabs have reached such a state
> That they are aiming at the Iranian imperial throne
> Fie upon thee, fie, O ever-turning Fortune![9]

Firdausī's scorn was preceded by some two centuries of the Shu'ūbīya movement in which the "wisdom" of the non-Arabs, the Greeks, Indians and, especially, the Iranians had been extolled, in contrast to the lack of culture of the Arabs. The Arabs, in return, claimed not only natural qualities but also that they were 'the first to produce Islam'.[10] But it was the ordinary Arab's very concept of Islam, with its emphasis on reward expected from God in afterlife for obeying Him in this world, that seemed to appeal to a far too selfish motive to be palatable to more cultured minds. Ultimately, its total rejection came from a defiant freed slave woman of Basra, an Arab city exposed to age-less Iranian influence. Rābi'a Baṣrī, who died in 801, had this saying attributed to her: "I am going to light a fire in paradise and pour water in hell, so that ... the servants of God may see Him without any object of hope or motive of fear."[11]

Stories are related of her scornful rejection of the gender-influenced theological tradition of Islam. One of these was told by a staid enough Sūfī, Shaikh Nasīruddin of Delhi, in 1354. Rābi'a Baṣrī, he said, was possessed of much beauty and grace. The principal men of Basra, consisting of scholars and mystics, resolved unanimously that this woman, while traversing the path of God, was wont to behave like a man; it might not happen that Satan led her astray. Thereupon they assembled together and went to Rābi'a. They told her, a woman however pious must have a husband. She asked the most learned of them to come forward. Upon Khwāja Ḥasan Baṣrī doing so, she asked him: "How was wisdom (*'aql*) divided, at Creation?" He replied, "Nine parts were given to men, one to women". And how, she went on, was lust (*shahwat*) divided. He said, "Contrary to that, nine parts of it were given to women, and just one to men." Rābi'a thereupon countered: "One-tenth of wisdom that I possess prevails over nine-tenth of lust that I have got, while the nine-tenths of wisdom that you people have cannot prevail over just one-tenth of lust!"[12] Presumably, she then bade them off.

If one were to disregard both the expectation of reward

and the fear of punishment, as motives for carrying out God's ordinances, then only the love of God, without any selfish object attached to it, could serve as the sole reason for doing so. Thus Rābi'a Baṣrī:

> 'I love thee with two loves, love of my happiness,
> And perfect love, to love Thee as is Thy due'.[13]

From this reliance on love alone, originated the entire ideological baggage of Sufism, or Muslim mysticism, which despite its acceptance of the *Sharī'at* as God's ordinances, saw God as a (female?) beloved and shunned the attractions of Paradise. In his conversations recorded in the first two decades of the fourteenth century, at Delhi, Shaikh Nizāmuddīn treated the seeker's pursuit of God on the analogy of an affair between two human lovers, with initial responses, estrangements, and reconciliations, but with the fearful possibility also present of an irrevocable breach.[14] A mystic is praised by him for giving away a divine order that released him from the fires of hell, or another who preferred hell rather than this world.[15] As the aim tended to turn away from merit (*ṣawāb*) with heaven as the object, to love aiming at communion or self-extinction (*fanā*), the final point of realization was summed up in the Persian mystic Manṣūr Hallāj's (857-922) exclamation, *an al-Ḥaqq*, 'I am God'. Though he was executed for this blasphemy, Hallāj remained a revered figure in *Sūfic* tradition.[16]

The exaltation of love over law took its boldest form in Persian poetry. In this, the 'idol' (*but*) became the symbol for both God and the human beloved; and 'idol-worship', which was so reviled in traditional Islam, became the main pursuit of the poet. Thus Amīr Khusrau (d.1325), held to be India's greatest Persian poet, asserted:

People say, 'Khusrau engages in idol-worship (*but parastī*).
Yes, yes, I do. No care have I for the people of the world.[17]

The entire tradition was carried from Persian into nineteenth-century Urdu poetry. One need only quote two couplets, one from Mīr Taqī 'Mīr', the other from Momin.

Mīr: What do you now ask of Mīr's faith and religion.
He has drawn the forehead-mark (*qashqa*) and sat in the temple, having forsaken Islam long ago.[18]

Momin: O Allāh, what a heresy! Abandoning the idol and the idol-house (*but o butkhāna*),
Momin is now setting off to Ka'ba, in the company of a pious person![19]

Inevitably, the glamour of heaven too dimmed for the poet. In a famous couplet Hāfiẓ (d.1391) exalts nature's beauty and man's handiwork over what God could offer in Paradise:

Give me, *sāqī*, the remaining wine, for in heaven you shall not find.
This bank of the Ruknābād river or the Musallā Garden.[20]

In Urdu with his usual frankness, Ghālib (d.1869), says all:

We know the reality of Paradise; but,
Ghālib, the idea is good to keep one's heart content.[21]

There was yet another notion taken into Persian poetry from Sufism, to justify departure from orthodox belief and practice. This was the concept of *pīr* or spiritual preceptor. By the fourteenth century absolute submission to the *pīr* had become so much a necessity for seekers on the mystic path that Nizāmuddīn denigrates the *ḥajj* pilgrimage (as a rival to visiting the *pīr's* hospice) and raises the *pīr's* grave to a higher position than the *Ka'ba*.[22] Amīr ḤHasan Sijzī, a poet and recorder of Nizāmuddīn's conversations, is the author of this verse:

> Every race of people have their own way, faith and object of prayer I have set right my prayer-direction (*qibla*) towards the awry-capped one.[23]

Here the "awry-capped one" could be the human beloved or, as Jahāngīr held, the *pīr*.[24] It gave rise to the curious concept of *pīr-i mughān*, a wine-seekers' preceptor, with Sufic authority. And so Hāfiẓ:

> Colour the prayer-carpet with wine, if the *Pīr-i mughān* so tells you;
> For the seeker should not be unaware of the road and custom of the journey's stages.[25]

If Sufic thought and custom led to these disturbing by-ways, there was still one streak in Islamic orthodoxy, which it accepted, namely, its professedly uncompromising monotheism, its belief in the absoluteness of God's authority, in His full knowledge of everything, and in the reality of predestination. But how could all this accord with the elabourate system of prayer, minutely defined ritual, the counting of merit (*ṣawāb*) for reward in afterlife, and the immense theological structure in which the ulema and the Sufis both believed? For would not such structures bind God's hands?[26] Any such restriction, even if voluntary on God's part, seemed to restrict His sway. The concept, therefore, arose of the pure monotheist (*muwaḥḥid*), who rejected every ritual and theology and believed only in God and in ethical conduct for its own sake and nothing else.

In the sixteenth century, Kabīr came to represent the model *muwaḥḥid*, and he is so designated by Abū'l Fazl (1595), who further noted that he had abandoned "the obsolete customs of the world" and held "both Muslims and Hindus as friends out of his broad-mindedness and elevated views".[27] What is striking is that *'Abdu'l Ḥaqq Muḥaddiṣ*, a younger contemporary of Abū'l Fazl and a scholar of impeccable orthodoxy, should also have recognized that *muwaḥḥids* were a race apart. He tells us that his father, when a child, asked his grandfather. "This famous Kabir, whose *bishanpads* are sung, was he a Muslim or an unbeliever (*kāfir*)?" He replied, "He was a *muwaḥḥid*." To the further query, whether a *muwaḥḥid* is "other than an unbeliever and Muslim", the reply was: "To understand this matter is difficult; you will (later) understand."[28]

There were, by the tenth century, two aspects of Islamic orthodoxy which had through a long process of continuous theological propaganda, seemingly secured immunity from fundamental criticism, first, the *Sharī'at*, or the legal framework, established by the major juridical schools, all going back to the ninth century, though it was recognized by Indian writers like Ziyā Baranī (fl.1350) that it was not in the sovereign's interest to enforce some parts of it.[29] The second was the rejection of rationality and science, against whose votaries both the influential Ghazālī (d.1111) and the Sūfīs had thrown their weight and for whom the historian Baranī too had reserved particular venom.[30]

Both these basic elements of orthodoxy, however, came into question during the reign of Akbar (1556-1605). Akbar had views on social matters that contrasted severely with the provisions of the *Sharī'at*. This was because of his belief in the inequity of slave-trade and slavery, his endorsement of daughters' full right to inheritance, his prohibition of child-marriage, and his advocacy of monogamy for the common mass.[31] This could only be justified if it was conceded that the *Sharī'at* was lamentably deficient in these areas. 'Abdu'l Qādir Badāūnī, in fact, reports Akbar's minister and main intellectual spokesman, Abū'l Fazl, as telling him, "If the Great Imām (Abū Ḥanīfa) had lived in our times, he would have written a different law-code (*fiqh*)."[32]

This revulsion against tradition (*taqlīd*) was combined with a new enthusiasm for reason and science. Not only does Abū'l Fazl argue that a sovereign "should not seek popular acclaim through opposing reason,"[33] but Akbar himself is said to have pronounced firmly that "the case for pursuing reason (*'aql pazhohī*) and rejection of traditionalism (*taqlīd*) is so clear that it does not need any argument from me."[34] In a conversation with a theologian Shaikh Aḥmad Sirhindi, Abū'l Fazl began praising the philosophers and their learning. Thereupon Shaikh Ahmad could not restrain his 'fervour (*junūn*) for Islam' and quoted Imām Ghazālī's assertion that some sciences are derived from books of prophets, while the rest are of no use for the faith. To all this Abū'l Fazl replied shortly, "Ghazālī spoke nonsense (*nāma'qūl*)."[35]

In their challenge to the legal structure and anti-philosophical stance of orthodox Islam, Akbar and his circle drew heavily on the pantheistic (or quasi-pantheistic) doctrines of the Sufic teacher Ibn 'Arabī (d.1240). The transmission of his ideas to India by Akbar's time has been well traced by S. Athar Abbas Rizvi;[36] and their conveyance to Akbar himself is also duly recorded.[37]

Whatever might be the range of complexities and by-lanes in Ibn 'Arabī's original message, at Akbar's court, it was treated as one of practically unalloyed pantheism, except for one characteristic twist now introduced into it. While God has created a universe of illusion (*ghubār*, 'misty dust'), which embraces both religion (*dīn*) and the world (*dunyā*), God Himself is described essentially as "the giver of world-ornamenting reason (*khirad-bakhsh-i jahān ārā*)".[38] It followed from this vision of the universe that all religions and sects being themselves illusory must be tolerated, under the principle of *ṣulḥ-i kul* (absolute peace); but still more so was this protection to be given to reason, seen as a special gift from God.[39]

This use of a Sufic theory to justify a policy of exalting reason and promoting tolerance of all religions was an innovation, which could only cause bitter controversy with the Muslim orthodoxy.[40] But it is possible that some of the ideas promoted by Akbar and his circle were also unconsciously adopted by his bitterest critics. Of this we find evidence even in Badāūnī's *Najātu'r Rashīd* (c.1595), a work on ethics professedly based upon the *Sharī'at*.

The author, a notorious critic of Akbar, is naturally conservative in his ethics, anxious to take the strictest positions. And yet there are unexpected deviations. Shaikh Aḥmad Sirhindī deemed it to be a great favour shown by God to men that they can marry four women, cohabit with any number of concubines and "use divorce to change their wives (*nisā*)."[41] Badāūnī does not reach these depths, and, indeed, lets his humanity prevail over the permissiveness of the *Sharī'at*. He expressly commends Indians for shunning the practice of divorce, and considering the word 'divorcer' (*ṭalāqī*) as the worst possible term of abuse.[42] At another place he records a saying of the Prophet: "Allah curses anyone who slaughters a cow, cuts down a tree and sells a human being." Badāūnī concedes that there is some doubt about the genuineness of this *ḥadīṣ* (tradition), but still commends it. He, then, goes on to say: "The common belief of the people now is that unless they eat cow's meat, their faith [in Islam] is not established. And the fact that [Muslim] recluses and ascetics avoid eating animal meat and eat grain and seed, carries no weight with them. God be praised! What a spectacle it is where Islam has got to."[43] The famous theologian Shāh Waliullah (d.1762) gloried in the thought of how non-Muslims would be kept in absolute misery, as hewers of wood and drawers of water, in an Islamic state.[44] Badāūnī, however, in a remarkable aside, envisions a partnership. The *kāfirs*, he says, are "also partners with us in worldly dealings, whether of profit or loss, for, although they do not belong to our professing community (*ummat-i ijābat*), they belong to the invited community (*ummat-i da'wat*) and the invitation of our Great Prophet, peace be on him, is extended to all human beings, from east to west, including the genii".[45]

The ideas that sprouted under Akbar's patronage were long-lasting in their influence. His son Jahāngīr (1605-27) would tax Muslim theologians with the question as to how they could deem as cancelled the Quranic verse, *lakum dīnakum wali-a dīn* ('To you your religion, to me mine'). On another occasion Jahāngīr wished "God would protect all his creatures from the disease of bigotry" (*ta'aṣṣub*).[46] Jahāngīr is also important because by his association with Chitrarūpa (Jadrūp), he recognized a compatibility between Sufic pantheism and Advaita Vedānta.[47]

It is noticeable, however, that in this spiritual encounter there is no longer the same emphasis on reason, that had been such a marked feature of the religious thought of Akbar and Abū'l Faẓl. Partly, perhaps, this might have been due to the fact that neither monotheism nor pantheism could be rationally justified, as the ever sceptical Ghalib was to put so well in verse, more than two centuries later.[48] It was, therefore, inevitable, perhaps, that the discourse on pantheism now shifted purely to the realm of faith, and was now bereft of practically all the social implications that had been earlier drawn from it.

This shift is best seen in Dārā Shukoh (d.1659), who in his introduction to his momentous Persian translation of the Upanishads (1657), insists that the pantheism he reads in these ancient texts derived from God's discourse (*kalām-i ilāhī*) and scriptural texts (*kutub-i samāvī*).[49] In such an interpretation of the Qurān, seeking in it particularly a reference to the Upanishads themselves, Dārā Shukoh defied the entire body of Muslim theological opinion. Of this he took little account, for he wrote:

> "Paradise is the place where there is no mullah and so no disputation and noise from the mullah".

And

> "In a city where a mullah resides
> No wise man can live".[50]

From the quotations of Urdu poets, Mīr, Momin and Ghālib already given in the main text and footnotes, it would be apparent that, notably in the *ghazal* form of Urdu poetry, a tradition of defiance and scepticism with regard to established orthodox custom and belief was distinctly in existence by the earlier part of the nineteenth century. It is a matter to consider whether, the Rebels of 1857 did not also draw on this tradition to justify an alliance against the English, crossing religious barriers. A rich source for this is the rebel weekly *Dehli Urdū Akhbār*. It directly countered the argument that the Muslims, as directed by their religion, should not rebel because they had no *imām* (a favourite

Wahhābī thesis) and should rather join the English, 'the People of the Book', in killing the Hindus.[51] In a further issue it invoked Shaikh Sa'dī's dictum, "Human beings are limbs of one another," to declare that the cause of Hindus and Muslims was inseparable.[52]

With Syed Ahmad Khan (d.1898), an official, who played his due part as a junior official in loyally supporting the English in 1857, we enter a new phase where orthodox Islam had to face the impact of modern ideas and values. Increasingly this led Syed Ahmad Khan to argue, that since the "Word of God" (the Quran) could not be in conflict with the "Work of God" (science), the Quran must be subjected to a constant process of re-interpretation. A large part of the *Ḥadīṣ* (the Prophet's reported statements) must also be rejected. No supernatural events ('miracles') were possible, whether by the Prophets or by others. Monogamy, not polygamy, was the practice really enjoined.[53]

In view of the opposition aroused against Syed Ahmad Khan's views, they are hardly ever recalled in current theological controversies. Abū'l Kalām Āzād, seeking to meet both the demands of rationality and the needs of human reconciliation (from the standpoint of the Indian National Movement) left his *Tarjumānu'l Qurān* (Urdu translation of the Qurān, with commentary) incomplete. In effect, modern religious reinterpretation of Islam has proved abortive and largely unconvincing, to the believers. It may seem, then, that we have reached a point where it is no longer possible to accommodate modern human values in any religious framework whatsoever; and reason and science must at long last stand on their own.

NOTES

1. "Religion is the sigh of the oppressed creature, the heart of a heartless world. It is the opium of the people" (Marx, 'Contribution to the Critique of Hegel's Philosophy of Right', 1844, in K. Marx and F. Engels, *On Religion*, Foreign Languages Publishing House, Moscow, 1957, p. 42).
2. I remember how Dr. Ashraf, during a visit to Aligarh in the 1950s, spent hours poring over the Arabic text of the *Fatāwāi 'Ālamgīrī*, brushing aside my suggestion that he use the Urdu translation of the work, which was more conveniently available.
3. For a balanced treatment of the Mu'tazilite 'heresy', see H.A.R. Gibb, *Mohammedanism: An Historical Survey,* London, 1953, pp. 107-18.
4. K.A.C. Creswell, *A Short Account of Early Muslim Architecture*, Harmondsworth, 1958, p. 18.
5. Edward C. Sachau, tr., *Alberuni's India*, London, 1910, Vol. II, p. 161. He is, however, realistic enough to recognize that even Christians were unable to follow the principle once Constantine the Great put them in power.
6. See e.g. *Alberuni's India,* I, pp. 29-30.
7. Ibid., I, p. 44.
8. Cf. Sachau in *Alberuni's India,* I, pp. xli-xlii.
9. *Zi shīr-i shutar khwurdan o sūsmār,*
'Arab rā bajāi rasīdast kār
ki Takht-i Kayān rā kunand ārzū
tafū bar tū, ai charkh-i gardān, tafū
10. See the classic study of this controversy in Ignaz Goldziher, *Muslim Studies* (English transl., ed. M. Stern with introd. by Ḥamīd Dabashi, New Brunswick, pp. 137-63.
11. Cyril Glasse, *The Concise Encyclopaedia of Islam,* revised ed., London, 2001, p. 376. Numerous versions of this famous assertion exist.
12. Ḥamīd Qalandar, *Khairu'l Majālis*, ed. Khaliq Ahmad Nizami, Aligarh, 1959, pp. 200-01. The passage has been slightly abridged in my rendering here.
13. R.A. Nicholson's transl. from Arabic, quoted in H.A.R. Gibb, *Mohammedanism*, p. 133.

14. Amīr Ḥasan Sijzī, *Fawā'idu'l Fawād*, ed. M. Latif Malik, Lahore, 1966, pp. 26-7. See also pp. 90 , 408.
15. Ibid., pp. 93, 140.
16. Ibid., p. 431.
17. *Khalq mī goyad ki Khusrau but-parastī mī-kunad*
    Āre! Āre! Mī kunam, bā khalq-i 'Ālam kār nīst.
18. *Mīr ke dīn o mazhab ko tum pūchhte kyā ho, unne to*
    Qashqa khenchā, dair men baiṭhā, kab kā tark Islām kiyā.
19. *Allāh re gum-rahī! but o butkhāna chhoṛ kar,*
    Momin chalā hai Ka'be ko, ek pārsā ke sāth.
20. *Bideh sāqī maye bāqī, ki dar Jannat na-khwāhī yāft*
    Kinār-i āb-i Ruknābād o gulgasht-i Muṣallā rā.
21. *Ham ko ma'lūm hai Jannat kī ḥaqīqat, lekin*
    Dil ke khwush rakhne ko yeh khyāl achchhā hai.
22. *Fawā'idu'l Fawād*, pp. 99, 362-3.
23. *Har qaum rā'st rāhe, dīne o qiblagāhe*
    Man qibla rāst kardam bar simt-i kaj-kulāhe.
    This couplet has often been wrongly attributed to Amīr Khusrau, the emperor Jahāngīr, being perhaps the first to fall into this error (see reference in following footnote).
24. Jahāngīr, *Tuzuk-i Jahāngīrī*, ed. Syed Ahmad Khan, Aligarh, 1863-64, p. 81.
25. *Ba-mai sajjāda rangīn kun, agar pīr-i mughān goyad.*
    Ki sālik be-khabar nabwud zi rāh o rasm-i manzilhā
26. It was this possibility of interference with predestination that allowed the Urdu poet Iqbāl (d.1938) to say:
    Raise your Self so high that before every turn of fate
    God may ask his slave (i.e. you), 'Tell me, what is your wish?'
    (*Khwudī ko kar buland itnā ki har taqdīr ke pahle*
    Khudā bande se khwud pūchhe, 'Batā terī raẓā kyā hai?'
27. Abū'l Faẓl, *Ā'īn-i Akbarī*, ed. H. Blochmann, Bib. Ind., Calcutta, 1867-77, I, pp. 393, 433.
28. 'Abdu'l Ḥaqq, *Akhbāru'l Akhyār*, Deoband, n.d., p. 306. The passage occurs in the last chapter (*takmila*) and the date of the conversation is given in the Hijri equivalent of February 19, 1522.

Ghālib's assertion, "We are *muwaḥḥids,* our religion is the abandonment of all custom (*rusūm*)" (*ham muwaḥḥid hain, hamārā kesh hai tark-i rusūm*) has thus a respectable niche in past Islamic thought.

29. Baranī, *Fatāwā-i Jahāndārī,* Indian Office (London) MS I.O. 1149 Ethe I, 2563), ff.8a-9a, for the general enforcement of the *Sharī'at*; and for exceptions, his *Tārīkh-i Fīrozshāhī,* ed. Saiyid Ahmad Khan, & c., Bib. Ind., Calcutta, 1860-62, p. 43.
30. For Sufic hostility to science and philosophy, see *Fawā'idu'l Fawạd*, pp. 84-6, 283-4, recalling a silly anecdote about Fārābī and Shihābuddīn Suhrawardī. For Baranī's diatribes, see *Fatāwā-i Jahāndārī,* I.O. 1149, ff 9b-10b; *Tārīkh-i Fīrozshāhī,* Bib., Ind., pp. 265-6.
31. Cf. Irfan Habib, 'Akbar and Social Inequities', *Proceedings of the Indian History Congress,* Warangal Session (1993), pp. 300-10.
32. Badāūnī, *Muntakhabu't Tawārīkh,* ed. Ali, Ahmad and Lees, Bib. Ind., Calcutta, 1864-9, III, p. 79.
33. Abū'l Faẓl, *Ā'īn-i Akbarī,* ed. H. Blochmann, I, p. 3.
34. Ibid., II, p. 229.
35. Hāshim Kishmī, *Zubdatu'l Maqāmāt,* litho., Kanpur, 1890, pp. 131-2. The author says the conversation was reported to him by someone present. Shaikh Aḥmad turned into a Sūfī later.
36. S.A.A. Rizvi, *Muslim Revivalist Movements in Northern India in the Sixteenth and Seventeenth Centuries,* Lucknow, 1965, pp. 31-67.
37. Badāūnī, *Muntakhabu't Tawārīkh,* II, pp. 258-9.
38. *Ā'īn-i Akbarī,* ed. Blochmann, I, p. 158. This opening passage of the chapter *Ā'īn-i Rahnamūnī* has been quite inaccurately rendered in Blochmann's own translation of the *Ā'īn-i Akbarī,* revised by D.C. Phillott, Calcutta, 1927, pp. 170-71.
39. For Akbar's religious ideas see Shireen Moosvi, 'The Road to Sulh-i Kul', in: Irfan Habib (ed.), *Religion in Indian History,* New Delhi, 2007, pp. 167-76; M. Athar Ali, *Mughal India, Studies in Polity, Ideas, Society and Culture,* New Delhi, 2006, pp. 158-72; and Iqtidar Alam Khan, 'Akbar's Personality Traits and World Outlook', in: Irfan Habib (ed.), *Akbar and His India,* New Delhi,

1997, pp. 79-96.

40. See the remarks of the contemporary biographer of Indian Sufis, Muḥammad Ghauṣī Shattārī, *Gulzār-i Abrār,* ed. M. Zaki, Patna, 1997, p. 277.

41. *Maktūbāt-i Imām Rabbānī,* Vol. I, Letter No. 192, to 'Abdu'r Rahīm Khān-i Khānān. There are different editions of this work, so it is best to cite the letters by their numbers.

42. *Najātu'r Rashīd,* ed. S. Moinul Haq, Lahore, 1972, pp. 436-37.

43. Ibid., p. 264.

44. *Hujjat Allāh al-Bāligha,* ed. Abu Muhammad Abdul Haq Haqqani, Karachi, n.d., I, p. 257.

45. *Najātu'r Rashīd,* p. 201.

46. 'Abdu's Sattār, *Majālis-i Jahāngīrī* (Conversations of Jahāngīr), ed. Arif Naushahi and Moeen Nizami, Tehran, 2006, pp. 78, 121-2, 124-6.

47. Cf. Shireen Moosvi, 'The Mughal Encounter with Vedanta: Recovering the Biography of "Jadrūp"', *Proceedings of the Indian History Congress* (61st Session, Kolkata, 2000-01), pp. 441-52.

48. (A) "When there was nothing, there was God; had I been nothing, I would have been God.
My (turning into a) being has sunk me; had I been nothing, what would I have been!"

(B) "When other than Thee, there is nothing,
Then, O God, whatever is all this tumult?"

[A] *"Na thā kuchh to Khudā thā, kuchh na hotā to Khudā hotā
Duboyā mujh ko hone ne, na hotā main to kyā hotā!"*

[B] *"Jab tujh bin nahīn ko'ī maujūd, phir ye hangāma,
ai Khudā, kyā hai?"*

49. Dārā Shukoh, *Sirru'l Asrār.* I am quoting here from a manuscript, though the work has been printed.

50. Dārā Shukoh, *Dīwān-i Dārā Shukoh,* ed. Ahmad Nabi Khan, Lahore, 1969, pp. 54-5. The couplets are:

*"Bihisht ānjā ki mullā'e nabāshad
Zi mullā baḥṣ o ghaughāi nabāshad
Dar ān shahre ki mullā khāna dārad
Dar ān-jā hech dānāe nabāshad."*

51. *Dehli Urdū Akhbār*, July 5, 1857. The paper printed the full text of a British appeal (*ishtihār*) to Muslims, put up at the Jāmi‘ Masjid at Delhi, and then replied to it point-by-point.

52. Ibid., July 19, 1857. Sa‘dī's words are: "*Banī Ādam a'zā'i yak-dīgar and.*"

53. The most detailed work on Syed Ahmad Khan's thought and religious writings is Christian W. Troll, *Sayyid Ahmad Khan, A Re-interpretation of Muslim Theology*, New Delhi, 1978. One could argue that what Syed Ahmad Khan aimed at was, in effect, a rejection, rather than a re-interpretation of the main elements of Muslim theology. He boldly restated his views in his correspondence with Mahdi Mohsinul Mulk in 1892 (printed as Sayyid Ahmad, *Taḥrīr fī uṣūl al-Tafsīr,* Agra, 1892). In this pamphlet, among other things, he points out the necessity of re-interpreting the words of the Quran in view of the Copernican theory (pp. 61-2).

3

Making Laws, Breaking Laws: Brahmanical and Buddhist Perspectives from Early India

Kumkum Roy

The focus of the present seminar, in memory of Professor K.M. Ashraf, on *Authority and Challenge: Processes of State and Social Formation in India,* is at once daunting and exciting. This is especially so given our often paradoxically painful location within universities. At one level, and inherently, universities are hierarchical institutions; we are reminded of this periodically, if not constantly through the ways in which decisions are taken as well as what is decided. And yet, at the same time, universities have remained, and hopefully will continue to remain spaces of debate, dialogue, discussion; of creative thinking that has often led to interventions in the world around us, even as we are implicated in it. Occasionally, when the inexorable weight of university hierarchies weigh us down, it is useful to remind ourselves that there have been situations, both past and present, in which alternative modes of envisaging regulation and social relations have coexisted. This is not to say we must learn from the past in any direct sense, but to explore the possibility of creating space to think through and with the past, or pasts, amongst a range of other options.

In order to illustrate the possibilities of such an engagement, I will discuss how law making was envisaged in the early Indian context, drawing on two texts—the *Manusmrti,* in Sanskrit, often regarded as the classic example of the enunciation of Brahmanical *dharma*, and the *Vinaya Pitaka*, located within the Pali Buddhist tradition.[1]

Both these texts are complex, and are located within distinctive traditions of composition and transmission. However, for the present, I would like to draw attention to some of their contents, rather than to these contexts, important as they are for acquiring a sense of multiple meanings. There are three interrelated issues that I will attempt to address—how is the making of laws or rules visualized in these texts; what is defined as the legitimate sphere for such 'legislation' and what are the kinds of rewards and punishments that are envisaged for conforming to these provisions and/or deviating from them. What emerges from the comparison may not yield direct insights into processes of state and social formation in early India, but can provide us with a sense of the complexities involved in arriving at an understanding of these issues.

The *Manusmrti*, for better or worse, is a text that most of us have heard about, if not read and studied. According to recent scholarship, most notably that of Olivelle,[2] it was probably compiled in the second century CE. It was composed in Sanskrit verse, in the *anustubh* metre. This metre lends itself to easy memorization, and was used extensively in texts such as the *Ramayana, Mahabharata* and the Puranas.

The *Vinaya Pitaka* is one amongst three texts recognized as canonical within the early Buddhist tradition, which holds that it was compiled in the First Buddhist Council, believed to have been held a hundred years after the death of the Buddha. Some of its earliest segments may date to the time of the Buddha, though the compilation as a whole can probably be assigned to the turn of the first millennium BCE/CE. It is composed in prose, and includes dialogues, a feature to which we will return, and consists of the rules that were expected to govern the conduct of members of the monastic community.

Both the *Manusmrti* and the *Vinaya Pitaka* lay down,

although in very different ways, the means whereby a distinctive identity could be constituted. As scholars such as Doniger3 have pointed out, the *Manusmrti* both implicitly and explicitly seems to have been composed by and for *brahmanas.* In other words, while the text was widely disseminated, there are several provisions that indicate that the intended audience consisted mainly if not solely of *brahmanas.* I will cite just one of many instances of this. This is from the discussion on hospitality, which lays down who should be considered as a guest and who should not. I quote approximately (MS III. 102-104):

> According to the *smrti*, a guest is a *brahmana* who spends just one night. He is called *atithi* because his stay is brief. A *brahmana* living in the same village or on a social visit cannot be considered a guest even when he comes to a house which has a wife or even the sacred fires. When the foolish householders become attached to other people's cooking, the result is that after death they are born as the cattle of those who gave them food.

In other words, it suggests that the *brahmana* alone could be a guest, either good or bad; the possibility of other men (or women) being considered as guests does not even arise, from this perspective.

Similarly, the *Vinaya Pitaka* was geared towards constituting and maintaining the identity of the Buddhist monk. We find a preoccupation with details that are often mind boggling, with the externals that would allow a man to be identified as a monk by others. These include lengthy discussions on the kinds of robes to be worn, footwear, the alms bowl to be carried on the begging round. There are also equally detailed discussions on life within the monastery—how bedding should be kept, how monks should behave towards one another, etc. And inevitably, in both texts we find an 'other' or sometimes several 'others'. Thus, while it is true that the *Manusmrti* is at one level concerned with constructing an image of a larger social if not cosmic universe, and the focus of the *Vinaya Pitaka* may seem relatively narrow, we can also suggest that there were certain common concerns in terms of questions of identity, and use this as an entry point into our discussion.

We may also note that our discussion on the texts is merely illustrative—both texts are rich and complex and deal with a range of issues that cannot be adequately addressed within the scope of the present paper. My attempt is to focus on some issues for comparison rather than provide an exhaustive analysis of either of these texts.

Preludes to Formulating the Law

Let us note how the *Manusmrti* begins: Manu, the primeval man, was seated, when the great sages, the *maharsis*, approached him with a request that he enlighten them about the *dharma* of all the *varnas* (MS I.1-2). This is because he was regarded as omniscient (MS I.3). This is followed by an account of how the world came into existence, including a reiteration of the well-known hierarchies of the *Purusasukta* (MS.I.31), the *Rgvedic* hymn that describes the origins of the cosmos, in which the 'ideal' social order is embedded, with the *brahmana* emerging from the head, the *ksatriya* from the arms, the *vaisya* from the thighs and the *sudra* from the feet of the primeval man. What is noteworthy is that the pronouncements are framed in a top down mode—a plea is made to Manu, and he responds by making a series of pronouncements.

If the concern with the *varna* order resonates through

the text, it is not surprising to find the Vedas being invoked as sources of authority. And yet, they are not the only *dharma-mula*, root or source of *dharma*. Other sources include the practices of those identified as *sistas*, the good, as well as what leads to personal satisfaction (*atma-tusti*). The text also declares that the Vedas constitute sruti, or revealed knowledge, that which is heard, the Dharmasastra is *smrti*, that which is recollected or remembered, and neither of them should be called into question: it is on them that *dharma* rests (MS II.10). Any twice-born man who challenges this by resorting to logic, taking the help of *hetusastra*, is warned that he would be ostracized (*bahiskrta*), by the good (*sadhu*), regarded as a *nastika* or unbeliever, and a *vedanindaka*, someone who had abused the Vedas (MS II.11). One finds then that there is in the text an attempt to be flexible—at the same time, in the last resort, the sanctity of the Vedas is recognized as inviolable.

Several narratives in the *Vinaya Pitaka* discuss how and why certain rules were formulated. Almost invariably, the Buddha is invoked as the ultimate authority in such instances. And yet, his authority stems not from claims to divinity, but from an insight and wisdom that is at once mundane and compassionate. Consider, for instance, the following, one of many examples. This is a situation described in the *Mahavagga*, a part of the *Vinaya Pitaka* (*Mahavagga*, I.12.1-4). *Bhikkhus* would bring potential renunciates from distant lands so that they could be initiated by the Buddha. By the time they reached the Buddha, both the monks as well as the future initiates would be tired. Taking into consideration this situation, the Buddha thought:

> What if I were to grant permission to the Bhikkhus, saying: "Confer henceforth, O Bhikkhus, in the different regions,

> and in the different countries, the pabbagga on upasampada ordinations yourselves."

And then he proceeded to state this publicly, delivering a discourse that evening, allowing for this measure of decentralization, reflecting at once his trust in the organization that he had established, as well as a humane concern for the comfort, well-being and convenience of those who were or aspired to be his followers. From the Brahmanical perspective, this may have been regarded as an example of using *hetusastra* to create new possibilities, moving away from acknowledged authorities.

Yet another context for laying down laws that is frequently invoked is that of the intervention of lay people. One instance of this runs as follows. *Bhikkhus*, who lacked proper teachers, misbehaved when they went on their daily begging round—some did not wear clothes properly, others demanded food and "in the dining halls they made a great and loud noise." (*Mahavagga* I.25.1,2). The people, we learn "were annoyed, murmured and became angry... 'They behave like Brahmanas at the dinners given to them.'" The *bhikkhus* heard this, and, in due course, informed the Buddha about it. He enquired whether this was true and then went on to lay down rules to regulate the conduct of the monks.

Elsewhere, people protested when they found escaped prisoners joining the *samgha*, and the Buddha agreed to ensure that this did not happen in future (*Mahavagga* I.42.2). A similar provision, put in place after popular disapproval, led to the exclusion of debtors (*Mahavagga* I.46) and slaves, whose masters objected (*Mahavagga* I.47).

All these suggest an acceptance rather than a questioning of existing social norms and practices. At the same time, they are interesting because they suggest that there were no claims to an exclusive status for the members of the *samgha*; they were visualized as being implicated in the social world around them, with all its complications and tensions. This is perhaps best exemplified in the 'history' about the rules regarding the retreat, the cessation of wandering during the rainy season. We learn (*Mahavagga* III.1.2):

> People were annoyed, murmured and became angry, saying, 'How can the Sakyaputtiya Samanas go on their travels alike during winter, summer and the rainy season? They crush the green herbs, they hurt vegetable life, they destroy the lives of many small living things.

In response, the Buddha, to whom the message was communicated by the *bhikkhus*, decided to institute the practice of *vassa* (Ibid. III. 1.3), which involved staying at one place, chosen carefully, for the duration of the monsoons.

If this may appear as a major decision, the anonymous 'people' are also cited as being the moving force behind deciding what kind of footwear monks should use (*Mahavagga* V. 2). There seems to have been an almost unlimited variety available—blue, yellow, red, brown, black and orange, also, with all kinds of decorations—with ram's horn, goat hair, scorpion tails, peacock feathers, lion skin, tiger skin, panther skin, antelope skin, otter skin, cat skin, squirrel skin, owl skin —the people successfully object when the monks use any of these, as also to shoes decorated with grass, wool, gold, silver, pearls, crystal, glass, tin, lead and bronze.

In some instances, the laying down of specific precepts is attributed to named lay people. One of these is Jivaka Komarabhacca, one of the most renowned doctors of the time. Jivaka served both Bimbisara, the king of Magadha, and his obviously large royal household, as well as the *bhikkhus*, and found little time to look after ordinary men. Several of these men then decided to join the *samgha* to avail themselves of his services. What is more, one of them returned to his worldly existence after being cured. When Jivaka discovered this, he raised the matter with the Buddha, who, after due consideration, decided to prohibit the entry of such men into the *samgha* (*Mahavagga* I.39.7). Similarly, the intervention of the king Bimbisara, we learn, led the Buddha to deny men who were in royal service admission into the *samgha* (*Mahavagga* I.40. 4).

Other individuals whose opinions were considered to be influential in the formulation of the law included Visakha Migaramata. She, we learn (*Mahavagga* III.13.2)

> Was annoyed, murmured and became angry (saying), 'How can the noble ones make such an agreement that nobody shall receive the pabbagga ordination during the rainy season? At what time ought the duties of the Dhamma not to be performed?'

Expectedly, her opinion is conveyed to the Buddha, and prevails.

Contrast this with the virtual absence of similar contextualization in the *Manusmrti*. We find, for instance, what may seem to be perfectly unexceptionable rules, as for example those relating to daily matters of hygiene (MS IV.45-48):

He must never eat food wearing just a single garment, bathe naked, or urinate in a road, on ashes, in a cow pen, on ploughed land, into water, on to a mound or a hill, in a dilapidated temple, on to an ant hill, into occupied animal holes, while walking or standing, or in a river bank, or at the top of hill. He must never void urine or excrement facing the wind, a fire, a *brahmana*, the sun, water or cows.

Fairly unexceptionable, and generally sensible, though one wonders, or perhaps does not wonder why *brahmanas* were singled out amongst all the possible categories of men and women. What is also noteworthy is that we are not told why these provisions were considered necessary.

We find then, that rules within the *Vinaya Pitaka* were embedded in a putative context that justified their formulation in the first place and perhaps ensured their subsequent implementation as well. In the case of the *Manusmrti*, on the other hand, rules take the form of assertions that stand in solitary splendour, assertions that do not seem to require contextualization or justification, but derive their authority from the virtually divine author and his unquestionable insights.

Circulation of the Texts, Creating Communities

The *Manusmrti* describes itself as a *sastra*, a *sastra*, moreover, that is the preserve of *brahmana* teachers and students (MS I.102-103). The *Vinaya Pitaka* is also a somewhat exclusive text, meant for recitation and circulation amongst monks. The text, or at least certain sections of it, was meant to be recited every fortnight, to the entire community of monks, where those guilty of offences were expected to acknowledge their violations. At certain points in the recitation, the reciter was expected to pause, and repeat his question thrice—if there was silence, he would continue in the assumption that the monks were not guilty of the offence being discussed; in case they were guilty, this was an opportunity to come clear.

The *Vinaya Pitaka* was compiled with the objective of ensuring the smooth functioning of the community of monks. It is in this context that one notices a preoccupation with the minute details that could make or break a community. Thus, there are sections that deal with the acquisition of robes (*Vinaya Pitaka, Nissaggiya Pacittiya Dhamma*, 1-10),[4] seating (*Vinaya Pitaka, Pacittiya Dhamma*, 28),[5] and so forth. The length to which the text goes in specifying details is in itself enlightening. Here is just one example:

> Whatsoever Bhikkhu shall hide, or cause another to hide, a Bhikkhu's bowl, or his robe, or the mat on which he sits, or his needle-case, or his girdle, even though in fun—that is a *Pacittiya*. (*Vinaya Pitaka, Pacittiya Dhamma*, 60)[6]

This was not a serious offence, but nonetheless was classified as something that needed to be taken cognizance of.

As noted earlier, the stated preoccupation of the *Manusmrti* is with the *dharma* of all *varnas*, but from the perspective of the *brahmanas*. Within that there is a concern with a range of themes. One of these is regulation of the rites of passage or *samskaras*. These were developed as occasions for constituting and/or reinforcing identities. Of these *samskaras*, I will focus primarily on the *upanayana*, which marked the initiation of the young boy belonging to the first three *varnas* into studentship, a phase of acquiring Vedic learning, and compare this with provisions for studentship envisaged within the *Vinaya Pitaka*. There are common features in the texts, but also interesting differences. These indicate that there were different ways in which the relationship between the teacher and the taught could be put in place and regulated.

In the *Manusmrti*, the process of becoming and remaining a *brahmana* hinges on the performance of the *samskaras*, the more significant of which included the *upanayana* or initiation, which marked the second birth of the initiate. Initiation was hypothetically open to young boys belonging to the first three varnas, but was effectively confined to the *brahmanas*.[7] Initiation, moreover, was regarded as the true birth, leading to immortality, as opposed to physical birth, which was part of a more transient existence (MS II. 148).

Initiation, amongst other things, opened the way to the legitimate access to Vedic learning. In other words, it marked the beginning of studentship, encapsulated in the notion of *brahmacarya*, which was synonymous with male celibacy. Thus, the inbuilt exclusions (of women in general and *sudra* men in particular, and, implicitly, of all non-*brahmana* men), acquire significance. Access to the most prestigious forms of learning was then, by definition, restricted. These restrictions were developed even further by creating a list of ten—the son of the teacher, one who is obedient, one who provides (presumably other) knowledge, one who is *dharmika*, who is pure, who has given wealth, a good man, and someone who is related to the preceptor (MS II.109)—as being the ideal potential students.

The *Manusmrti* lays down the rules governing the student-teacher relationship in minute detail. The student was advised to regulate his senses as well as his external appearance and behaviour. For instance, we learn (MS II.194):

> In his teacher's presence, his food, clothes, and apparel should always be of a lesser quality than his teacher's. He should wake up before his teacher and go to bed after him.

Further (MS II. 195-198):

> He must never answer or converse with his teacher while

> lying down, seated, eating, standing, or facing away; he should do so standing up if the teacher is seated, approaching him if he is standing, going up to meet him if he is walking turned away form him, coming close to him if he is far away, and bending down if he is lying down or standing at a lower level. In his teacher's presence, he should always occupy a lower couch or seat; and within his teacher's sight, he must not sit as he pleases.

Thus, a sense of hierarchy was ingrained in virtually every aspect of communication between teacher and taught, leaving virtually no space for any subversion.

Contrast this with the situation envisaged in the *Vinaya Pitaka*. Here, the potential initiate was expected to make a deliberate conscious choice of joining the *samgha*. Also, the new initiate, known as the *saddhiviharika*, was expected to choose the teacher or the *upajjhaya* (*Mahavagga* I.25.7). The bond between the two was conceived in paternalistic terms, as between a father and a son. Yet, it is paternalistic without being condescending. We learn: "Thus these two, united by mutual reverence, confidence, and communion of life, will progress, advance, and reach a high stage in this doctrine and discipline" (*Mahavagga* I.25.6).[8]

At the same time, there is an element of subordination built into the daily routine that resonates with the Brahmanical precepts. This is spelt out in great detail—a sample runs as follows:

> Let him (i.e. the initiate) arise betimes, and having taken off his shoes and adjusted his upper robe so as to cover one shoulder, let him give the teeth-cleanser and water to rinse his mouth with. Then let him prepare a seat. If there is rice-milk, let him rinse the jug and offer the rice-milk. When he has drunk it, let him give water, take the jug, hold it down, rinse it properly without rubbing, and put it away. When the

> *upagghaya* has risen, let him take away the seat. If the place is dirty, let him sweep the place. (*Mahavagga* I.25.8)[9]

Yet, this subservience was not the only way in which the relationship was visualized. The *saddhiviharika* was expected to keep a watchful eye on, and if necessary restrain, the *upajjhaya* who was likely to commit an error. So for instance, we learn:

> If the upagghaya is in danger of committing an offence by the words he says let (the *saddhiviharika*) keep him back. (*Mahavagga* I.25.10)[10]

Further, it is stated (*Mahavagga*, I. 25.20):[11]

> If discontent has arisen with the *upagghaya*'s heart, let the *saddhiviharika* appease him, or cause him to be appeased (by another), or compose him by religious conversation. If indecision has arisen in the *upagghaya*'s mind, let the *saddhiviharika* dispel it or cause it to be dispelled, or compose him by religious conversation. If the *upagghaya* takes to a false doctrine, let the *saddhiviharika* discuss it, or cause another to discuss it, or compose (the *upagghaya*) by religious conversation.

And (*Mahavagga* I.25.21):[12]

> If the *upagghaya* is guilty of a grave offence and ought to be sentenced to *parivasa* discipline, let the *saddhiviharika* take care that the Samgha sentence the *upagghaya* to *parivasa* discipline.

The responsibilities of the *upagghaya* are also worked out at length (*Mahavagga* I.26.1-2):[13]

> If the *upagghay*a has an alms-bowl and the *saddhiviharika* has not, let the *upagghaya* give the alms-bowl to the saddhiviharika or take care that the *saddhiviharika* gets an alms-bowl.

If the *saddhivharika* is sick, let (the *upagghaya*) arise betimes and give him the teeth-cleanser and water to rinse his mouth with.

And (*Mahavagga* I. 26.11):[14]

> If the *saddhiviharika* is sick, let him nurse him as long as his life lasts, and wait until he has recovered.

In other words, while the relationship between the initiate and his preceptor was marked by carefully detailed gestures that underscored hierarchical relationships in both textual traditions, there was a significant difference as well. In the *Manusmrti*, there is no concern with real or potential situations of reciprocity or reversal within the relationship—the initiate was by definition in a perpetual state of subordination. The *Vinaya Pitaka*, on the other hand, envisaged a relationship of somewhat greater complexity—where, while the superiority of the preceptor was conceded, this was by no means unconditional or perpetual. The initiate was expected to keep a watchful eye on his master, and the latter in turn, was expected to take care of his disciple. Thus, the identities that may have been constituted through adherence to these rules may have been more fluid than those envisaged within the brahmanical tradition.

Rewards and Punishments, Inclusions and Exclusions

Let us turn, finally, to the stated objectives of the texts, and the traditions in which they were embedded, sustained through rewards and punishments. The *Manusmrti* assures us that the man who follows the law will attain fame, *kirti*, in this world, and unlimited happiness in the worlds beyond (MS II.9). The goal of the *Vinaya* is at once more limited and more exalted. On the one hand, the text was meant to ensure a harmonious existence within a carefully delimited community. On the other hand, successful participation in this community life was considered to be a necessary but not a sufficient condition for attaining the ultimate state of liberation, freedom from rebirth.

Entry into the community was, therefore, carefully regulated, and there were provisions for expulsion as well. Expulsion, was, in fact, the highest punishment envisaged. Four major offences were identified, each of which entailed expulsion from the *samgha*. These included indulging in sexual intercourse, stealing, killing or inciting to kill, and pretending to be more knowledgeable than one actually was (*Parajika Dhamma*, 1-4).[15]

Decisions in these and other matters had to be arrived at through consensus, but there was provision for voting as well. While this may appear as apparently simple and transparent, it was recognized that voting could be a contentious and complex process, whose validity could be challenged. Consider the following (*Cullavagga*, IV.10.1):

What are the ten [conditions] in which the taking of votes is invalid? When the matter in dispute is trivial, when the case has not run its course, when regarding the matter in dispute the Bhikkhus have not formally remembered or been formally called upon to remember the offence, when the taker of votes knows that those whose opinions are not in accordance with the law will be in the majority or probably may be in the majority, when he knows that the voting will result in schism—when he is in doubt whether the voting will result in schism, when the votes are irregularly given, when all do not vote equally, and when they do not vote in accordance with the view [which they really hold].[16]

While expulsion was this highest punitive measure that lay within the purview of the Buddhist *samgha*, there were also strategies of exclusion. Thus, we find that those who suffered from certain diseases—leprosy, boils, dry leprosy, consumption and fits, were denied admission (*Mahavagga*, I.39.7).[17] This list has interesting resonances with the list of families which men were asked to avoid in their search for brides, enumerated as follows in the *Manusmrti*: families prone to hemorrhoids, tuberculosis, dyspepsia, epilepsy, leucoderma or leprosy (MS III.7). Others who were excluded from membership of the *samgha* were debtors, slaves, prisoners, royal servants, as noted earlier, and the disabled (*Mahavagga* I.71.1).[18]

We may compare this with the detailed lists of men who were to be included or excluded from social intercourse, found in the *Manusmrti*, in the context of those who ought/ought not to be invited for the *sraddha* when offerings were made in honour of the dead male patrilineal ancestors. Evoking their memory was important to validate the continuity of the patrilineage as a social, economic and cultural entity. In this context, emphasis was laid on inviting the *srotriya*, the *brahmana* learned in the Vedas (MS III.128). The threat held out to deter the feeding of the ignorant *brahmana* is rather scary:

> A man will have to eat as many red hot spikes, spears, and iron balls as the rice balls that someone ignorant of the Vedas eats at his divine or ancestral offerings (MS III.133).[19]

What is also noteworthy is that the list of those who were to be excluded from the *sraddha* is much longer than the inclusions. The list consists of the *brahmana* who was a thief (*stena*), the *patita* or social outcaste, the *kliba* or person of indeterminate sex, the *nastika* who questioned the Vedas, the bald man, the gambler, one who performed sacrifices for a collective, the doctor, the temple priest, the seller of meat, the servant of a village or a king, a man with disfigured nails or teeth, the man who had abandoned his guru, one who had abandoned the sacrificial fire, an usurer, a man suffering from consumption, a pastoralist, a younger brother who married before his older brother, one who hated the Vedas, an older brother who married after his younger brother, actors, a *brahmacarin* who failed to maintain the vow of chastity, one married to a *sudra* woman, the son of a remarried woman, a one-eyed man, one who allowed his wife to take a lover, one who taught for a fee, one who learnt from such a teacher, one who had either a *sudra* as a disciple (*sisya*) or a guru, one of improper speech, the son of an adulteress, one who abandoned his father, mother or guru without reason, one who had social intercourse with the *patita*, one who burnt down houses, one who administered poison, one who ate the food of the son of an adulterous woman, one who sold *soma*, one who crossed the seas, a bard, an oil presser, one guilty of perjury, one who quarrelled with his father, a gambler, a drunkard, one suffering from an evil disease (*papa roga*), one who had committed a grave sin (*abhisasta*), a proud man, one who sold poison, a maker of bows and arrows, a lover of his elder sister-in-law, a betrayer of friends, one who earned his livelihood by gambling, who had been taught by his son, an epileptic, a man suffering from leucoderma, a liar, one who was insane, one who insulted the Vedas (*veda-nindaka*), one who trained elephants, horses, cattle and camels, an astrologer, one who reared birds, one who instructed in warfare, one who obstructed canals, an architect, a messenger or a gardener, one who used dogs for sport, a falconer, one who defiled a virgin, a cruel man, one who adopted the livelihood of a *sudra*, one who performed sacrifices for a multitude, one who did not follow custom, one who was neither male nor female, one who always asked for things, a farmer, one who had a club foot, one who was criticized by good people, one who kept sheep or buffaloes, the husband of a woman who was remarried, one who handled corpses (MS III. 150-166).

Another long list (MS IV. 217-221), this time of food that could not be accepted, runs as follows—food offered by the drunk, angry, and sick, food with hair or insects, food touched by the foot, that seen by a *bhrunaghna* (a term used both for one who killed a *brahmana* as well as for those who performed abortions), that touched by a menstruating woman, food pecked by a bird, touched by a dog, smelt by a cow, food given by a *gana* (a collective) or a *ganika* (sex-worker/courtesan), food despised by the learned (*vidusa*), food given by a thief, a musician, a carpenter, a usurer, a man consecrated for a sacrifice, a miser, a prisoner, an *abhisasta* (a man guilty of any one of the five major sins—killing a *brahmana* or a cow, stealing gold, violating the bed of a guru, drinking liquor, telling lies), food offered by someone of indeterminate sex, that offered by a *sudra*, leftovers, food offered by a doctor, that offered by a cruel man, that offered by a woman after childbirth, that offered by a liar, actor, tailor, blacksmith, hunter (*nisada*), goldsmith. The discussion ends by stating that consuming *rajanna* the food of the king, deprives one of *tejas* (spiritual power), the food of a *sudra* of *brahmavarcas* (the lustre typical of a *brahmana*), that of the *suvarnakara* or goldsmith of *ayus* (longevity) and that of the *carmavakartrin* or leather worker of *yasas* (fame).

How do we understand these long and meandering lists? We can draw attention to the principles of exclusion, which are diverse—these include occupations, perceived violations of socio-sexual norms, disabilities, violations or contestations of brahmanical ritual status. But what we also need to grapple with is what seems to be an underlying paranoia—an unending quest for ways and means of protecting the 'purity' of the *brahmana*. This anxiety probably stemmed from a situation where that 'purity' was being called into question.

Thus, we can suggest that strategies of inclusion and exclusion were common to both traditions, and that were overlaps in the concerns that emerge from a consideration of the underlying principles governing exclusions, in particular. This is not surprising, when we take into account the fact that both traditions emerged from a common milieu, and were in implicit, if not explicit dialogue with one another. However, what is noteworthy is that the this-worldly brahmanical tradition was as, if not more preoccupied with protecting social boundaries as the Buddhist monastic tradition, which was attempting to create an alternative social space.

Tentative Conclusions

We can notice then, certain similarities and differences between the Brahmanical and Buddhist endeavour. Both were preoccupied with defining legitimate members of the community/category. This task was by no means easy. For the Buddhist monk, it involved both distinguishing oneself from the laity through external markers such as the distinctive robe and begging bowl, as well as working out the basis for a communal existence. At the same time, relations with the laity were inevitable and complex. What is interesting is the space conceded to, and the authority assigned to the laity in framing rules, as recognized and textualized within the tradition. These included, as we have seen, some very important provisions such as that of the retreat for the period of the rainy season.

In contrast to the Buddhist negotiation, the non-Brahmanical voice finds no direct space in the *Manusmrti*. The non-brahmanical is viewed primarily as potentially disruptive, as posing a constant, almost infinitely diverse threat to the identity of the *brahmana*, a threat that could only partly be countered through the process of naming and enumerating. In other words, while the *brahmana* as envisaged in the *Manusmrti* was only occasionally a renunciate, and was more often than not ideally a part of the world around him, his identity seems to have been particularly fragile, requiring to be hedged in by definitions, and redefinitions, as well as reiterations. It also required additional bolstering by invoking divine support. In contrast to this, the Buddhist rules are represented as emerging through processes of dialogue, debate, and discussion, sometimes contentious, sometimes not. At the same time, and in spite of differences, there are interesting parallels in the enumerations of the major offences in both traditions, as well as in the lists drawn up of those who were to be excluded from social intercourse.

In this context, it is useful to remember that we also need to envisage, as has been suggested by Olivelle[20] and Fitzgerald,[21] amongst others, another level of dialogue—that between the Buddhist and the Brahmanical traditions in the post-Mauryan world. That might help us to make sense of the anxieties, as well as the resolutions, envisaged in the *Manusmrti* to safeguard identities that were being subjected to scrutiny, critique and interrogation both from those within the social order as well as from the order of renouncers. It may also help us understand the detailed inclusions and exclusions within the Buddhist *samgha*, in spite of the rhetoric of embracing everybody, and providing opportunities to attain the ultimate goal to all those who were genuinely engaged in the quest.

And we may then locate the specific provisions of the *Bhikkuni Vibhanga*, which emphasized the subordination of the order of women to that of men within the world of Buddhist remouncers, within a social order where the Brahmanical ideal of women attaining salvation through serving their husbands may have been fairly widespread. Rules then, emerged out of complex interactions, and were used to safeguard identities that could be subjected to scrutiny and critique, and needed constant reiteration in order to be accepted.

Where does this leave us as teachers and students, implicated in hierarchical institutions even as we may dream of more egalitarian alternatives? Is it possible to negotiate, to engage in dialogue, to work towards these ideals? Here, I would suggest, the *Vinaya Pitaka* offers certain possibilities, by suggesting that dialogues are necessary and even inevitable; dialogues amongst monks with starkly different points of views, between monks and the undifferentiated laity, between monks and significant laymen and women. It also opens possibilities of introducing new provisions, revisiting and even reversing earlier provisions in the light of new experience, grappling with the tension of creating a canon and capturing the messy fluidity of the everyday. This is not a world of the stark certainties and endless anxieties of the *Manusmrti.* And yet, there are hierarchies; between the Buddha and others, between men and women; between those who are included and excluded. It is useful then to remind ourselves that the past may not yield easy answers and directions, even as we may turn to it to open up possibilities for interrogating the present.

NOTES

1. All references to the *Manusmrti* are from Patrick Olivelle (ed. and tr.), *Manu's Code of Law, A Critical Edition of the Manava-Dharmasastra*, New Delhi, Oxford University Press, 2005. All references to the *Vinaya Pitaka* are for T.W. Rhys Davids and Hermann Oldenberg (tr), The *Vinaya Texts,* Parts I to III, Delhi, Motilal Banarsidass, 2008 (rpt, 1882, 1885). When citing from the translation, I retain the transliteration of Pali terms and names used by the translators. However, I modify the transliteration when using these terms and names elsewhere. For instance, the translation uses *upagghaya*, whereas I adopt *upajjhaya*.
2. Op. cit.
3. W. Doniger, (tr.), *The Laws of Manu,* London, Penguin, 1991.
4. Rhys Davids and Oldenberg, op. cit., Part I, pp. 18-24.
5. Ibid., p. 37.
6. Ibid., p. 46.
7. The other samskaras that were considered particularly significant included *vivaha*, or marriage, which marked the completion of Vedic learning and a formal recognition of the bridegroom as a potential householder who was expected to uphold both social and spiritual realms. And, while not a *samskara*, the *sraddha*, or the ritual respectful remembering of the dead, was also a crucial occasion for publicly demonstrating one's claims to status.
8. Rhys Davids and Oldenberg, op. cit., p. 154.
9. Ibid., pp. 154-5.
10. Ibid., p. 156.

11. Ibid., p. 161.
12. Ibid., p. 161.
13. Ibid., pp. 163-4.
14. Ibid., pp. 164-5.
15. Rhys Davids and Oldenberg, op. cit., Part I, pp. 3-6.
16. Rhys Davids and Oldenberg, op. cit., Part III, pp. 26-7.
17. Rhys Davids and Oldenberg, op. cit., Part I, p. 193.
18. Rhys Davids and Oldenberg, op. cit., Part I, pp. 224-5.
19. Olivelle, op. cit., p. 115.
20. Olivelle, op. cit, p. 40.
21. James L. Fitzgerald, *The Book of Peace*, Chicago, University of Chicago Press, 2004, pp. ix-x.

4

Leading Family Groups of the Mughal Mansabdars Under Shah Jahan

Firdos Anwar

The Mughal administration headed by the emperor was run by his 'nobility'—a convenient substitute for the medieval term, '*Umara*'. Their appointment, promotion, demotion and dismissal being the sole prerogative of the ruler, made the nobility fully dependent on him. Yet the significant role played by this group in implementing the king's policies and in administering the state, also made the ruler dependent on his nobility. Thus, besides the element of dependence, the element of inter-dependence too governed the nature of relationship between the two. It was because of this element of interdependence that cohesion between the two could be possible. This tendency of coherence flourished also because both of them thrived on the surplus produce of the land, yet there was an element of contradiction between the ruler and the nobility. And this was share in power.[1] Each of them tried to enlarge its share at the cost of the other. Whenever the king embarked on the policy of extreme centralization, the nobility generally, reciprocated with tough resistance.

These pulls and pushes drastically affected the fortunes of both during Humayun's times. A possible solution for this inherent problem was to maintain equilibrium between the elements of interdependence and contradiction. After attaining political maturity gradually, when Akbar defined his relations with his nobility afresh and demanded total submission from his nobles, he could not ignore the negative impact of the element of contradiction; therefore moving cautiously towards his goal, he decided to give some soothing concessions to the nobles, thereby maintaining equilibrium between the elements of interdependence and contradiction. That is why the penitent nobles were usually pardoned and reinstated in Mughal service. A sympathetic attitude was extended towards the family of a deceased noble by conferring mansab, *Wazifa, Khalat* and by usually distributing his property among his heirs after his death.[2] Such traditions served as guidelines for Akbar's successors and Shah Jahan too followed his grandfather as per his political wisdom. Besides forgiving the rebels and restoring mansab, in most of the cases he tried to be sociable with the nobles by visiting them at their *havelis* on different occasions.[3] Moreover the descendants of the mansabdars called *Khanazad*, were shown special favours generally. They were granted mansab after retirement, death or even during the lifetime of their ancestors. For example Muhammad Murad S/o Salabat Khan Roshan-Zamih was given a mansab of 500 *Zat*, 100 *Sawar* at the age of four years after the assassination of his father at the hands of Raja Amar Singh Rathor (in August 1644).[4] Similarly at the age of 11, Sa'dullah Khan's son, Lutfullah, got a mansab of 700 *Zat*, 100 *Sawar*.[5] Many more such cases may be cited to clarify the point that Shah Jahan took special care of the relatives of his mansabdars.

This speciality of the Khanazads is evident from their number. Duing 1628-36 out of the total of 342 mansabdars holding the rank of 1000 *Zat* and above, their number was 161 (47%).[6] Similarly during 1637-41, they were about 129 out of 255 (51%).[7] Their number further increased during 1642-58: 251 out of 448 (56%).[8] It may therefore be said that during Shah Jahan's reign, heredity carried much weight and Khanazads were the recipients of special favour.

This distinction attained by the Khanazads may not be

a unique phenomenon of the seventeenth century, but the emergence of some strong family groups, cutting across racial and religious lines, during Shah Jahan's reign was perhaps, an emphatic development. In some recent research works attention is paid to the rise and role of a few families under Akbar and Jahangir,[9] but such a study pertaining to Shah Jahan's period is still awaited. This paper is a primitive attempt to initiate such study with a direct reference to such issues like the identification of such family groups with the help of some primary sources; to determine the share of these families in the total awarded mansab; to examine the position of each group vis-à-vis its own racial group as well as among the rest of the family groups; to assess their position and role in key administrative positions, etc. Such a study would help in understanding the basic equation between Shah Jahan and these families. This could define the quantum of dependence between the two. Whether or not the rise of such family groups affected the element of equilibrium between the king and the nobility? Was there any negative impact of the emergence of such groups on the Mughal polity as such? Many more such queries are yet to be answered, at least tentatively. Our attempt to examine some of these propositions in a limited time frame could help in analysing the complexities of the crisis which finally led, not only to the showdown of arms between Shah Jahan and his nobility, but also resulted in his deposition and captivity—an incident which had no precedent in Mughal history so far.

At the very outset it should be clarified that for constructing the family lineage of the nobles we have mainly relied on *Zakhirat-ul-Khawanin* of Fareed Bhakkari and *Maasir-ul-Umara* of Shahnawaz Khan Safavi—the two authentic biographical dictionaries of the Mughal period. Secondly, for the sake of conciseness, we have focused on some leading families only. And finally, these family groups are evaluated in the periphery of the mansab; because mansab was the main apparatus to organize the nobility and to determine the status of its holder in the official hierarchy. The fixation of the salary and obligations of the nobility were also governed by the mansab. Last but not the least, mansab played a key role in regulating mutual relations between the king and his nobles. This study is confined only to the mansabdars of 1,000 *Zat* and above.

Irani Families

It would be justified to begin with the Iranis as they formed the single largest group in the nobility numberwise as well as mansabwise.[10] A positive role of the Iranis in the brief succession tussle before Shah Jahan's coronation, slightly indicated their ascendancy in the following regime. By putting Bulaqi (S/o Khusrau) on the throne to avoid the risk of its occupancy by a powerful person, Asaf Khan (later on Yamin-ud-Daulah) shattered the designs of Shahryar who had the blessings of Begum Nur Jahan, Asaf Khan's own sister.[11] He sent Banarsi, his confidant, to prince Shah Jahan in the Deccan with a word to reach the court as soon as possible.[12] Shaharyar, on the other hand, decided to fight for the throne—in fact to lose it forever. Out of about 26 nobles who fought for Shah Jahan, eight were the Iranis,[13] thus qualifying for greater favours in the near future. Immediately after the coronation when Shah Jahan rewarded his favourites, there were about 62 Iranis among the whole lot of about 176 mansabdars.[14] Thus from the beginning itself a greater degree of trust was deposited in them. And among all ethno-religious groups their lead was almost decided.[15]

In Table 1-A we have listed 24 leading Irani families along with their share in total mansab, awarded during the three phases of Shah Jahan's reign: 1628-36, 1637-41, 1642-58. These figures suggest the distinct position of Yamin-ud-Daulah's family as its share was the highest in both *Zat* and *Sawar* mansab.

These Irani families on the basis of their share in mansab, may be classified into three categories, namely, the recipients of tremendous favours like the families of Khalilullah Khan, Ali Mardan Khan, Islam Khan, Qazalbash Khan, Zulfiqar Khan and Zabardast Khan; in the second category we can include those who seem to have suffered in the total share, such as the families of Mahabat Khan, Khwaja Abul Hasan, Asaf Khan Jafar Beg, Afzal Khan and others; and finally those families who remained almost at the same level from wher they had started, like the families of Saif Khan Mirza Safi, Mirza Khan Manochahar, Qasim Khan Namkin and of Ilahwardi Khan.

To assess the position of these Irani families vis-à-vis their racial group as well as among all the family groups, information is provided in Table 1-B. The first interesting thing that emerges from this table is that during 1628-36, these families occupied more than half of the total *Zat* mansab held by this ethnic group, while in the total *Sawar* mansab of their racial group, their share was much larger—almost 76 per cent. In the succeeding phase, they further improved their share. However, in the last phase, these family groups had to suffer a marginal setback. Yet on the whole they seem to have enjoyed the largest share in the total mansab held by their racial group. Therefore it may be said that the distinctive ratio maintained by the Irani racial group in the total mansab award depended mainly on the share of their family groups.

Among the family groups too, the Iranis emerged as the strongest faction. In all the three phases they enjoyed about 38 per cent of *Zat* and about 40 per cent of *Sawar* mansab, collectively held by all the other families.

Turani Families

Although the ruling house belonged to the Turani stock and Shah Jahan was proud of being a Turani and adopted the title of 'Sahib Qiran-e-Sani', yet the Turani faction could not rise to the level of the Iranis. In the succession tussle they were less than the Iranis among Shah Jahan's supporters which accordingly curtailed their share in royal favours, given immediately after coronation. Out of 176 recipients of such favours only 26 were the Turanis (while the Iranis were 62). Yet they formed the second largest group of Shah Jahan's nobility.

Our study is confined to eight leading Turani families only. Their importance is evident from their share in mansab, shown familywise in Table 2-A. These figures suggest that Said Khan Zafar Jang's family was the foremost among them as it enjoyed the highest mansab both in *Zat* and *Sawar*. The remaining Turani families also improved their position throughout this period. This trend strengthens the position of Turani families vis-à-vis the Irani families; because unlike the Iranis, all the Turani families multiplied their share in mansab during all the three phases. It may also be noted that almost half of these families held greater *Sawar* mansab than their *Zat* mansab which implied greater reliance of the king. It may therefore be suggested that the Turanis were being gradually elevated at racial as well as family levels to counter balance the predominance of the Iranis.

Table 2-B provides relevant information pertaining to the total mansab award during the three phases, share of the Turanis as a racial group in it, total mansab held by the Turani families and the total mansab of all family groups, included in this study. These figures show that during 1628-36, Turani families shared almost 33 per cent of total *Zat* and 43 per cent of total *Sawar* mansab held by their racial group.

In the second phase (1637-41) there was a slight improvement in their share vis-à-vis their racial group, i.e. 38 per cent of the *Zat* and 50 per cent of the *Sawar*. The same trend seems to have prevailed during the last phase (1642-58) as their share rises to almost 44 per cent of the total *Zat* and more than 53 per cent of the total *Sawar* mansab held by them as a racial group. On these grounds one could say that unlike the Iranis whose greatest share in total awarded mansab mainly depended on the share of their families, the share of the Turanis in total mansab award largely depended on their identity as a racial group rather than a family group. Among the family groups too, they could hardly match the status of the Iranis.

Rajput Families

According to Farid Bhakkari, Akbar was advised by Humayun to treat the Rajputs with kindness and love because they were obedient and faithful. That is why, Farid observes, Akbar so favoured the Rajputs that it became a subject of comment.[16] Induction of this racial group in the Mughal nobility also helped Akbar in establishing a certain balance among various ethno-religious groups. A pro-Rajput policy thus became an established tradition and the Rajputs remained an integral part of the establishment till the effective Mughal rule in India. Show of Shah Jahan's favouritism for Muslim orthodoxy, evident from such concessions like the abolition of *Sajdah*, replacement of Zaminbos with *Chahar Taslim* and almost total liquidation of salutation in the case of Muslim religious heads, proved to be quite superficial as it could not affect any basic change in the nature of Mughal-Rajput relations during this period. They stood as the only leading group in Shah Jahan's nobility after the Iranis and the Turanis. Out of a total of 342 mansabdars 53 were Rajputs during 1628-36. Their position improved in the subsequent phase (1637-41) as they touched the figure of 41 out of 255. And finally (1642-58) their number reached 74 out of a total of 448. Their positive role in the succession tussle earned high favours for them. Out of 176 recipients of royal favour[17] in February-March 1628, 34 were Rajputs.

Rajput family groups may be placed next to the Iranis numberwise. Fifteen such families along with their mansab are listed in Table-3A. At a glance, one may notice the dominant position of the families of Rana Karan Raja Gaj Singh, Bir Singh Dev Bundela, Rao Ratan Hara and Raja Jai Singh in the first phase (1628-36). During the second phase (1637-41), with the exception of Raja Gaj Singh's family, all these groups had to lose in both *Zat* and *Sawar* mansab, which underlines the specialty of the house of Jodhpur. The greatest sufferer, however, was the family of Bir Singh Dev Bundela. Although not totally deprived of favour, the family certainly lost the prime position it enjoyed under Jahangir. Some of the Rajput families almost doubled their share in mansab by the end of this reign. Raja Gopaldas Gaur's family is a striking example of this kind. This family starting from 4,500 *Zat* and 3,000 *Sawar* reached the mansab of 15,000 *Zat* and 18,900 *Sawar* in the last phase (1642-58). The families of Kishan Bhadoriya, Raja Basu, Rawal Ponja, etc. may also be included in this category.

The third phase seems to be the most fertile period for the Rajput families as almost all of them gained considerably in mansab. However the gains of the families of Rana Karan, Gopal Das Gaur and Raja Gaj Singh had no parallel in the whole lot. Bir Singh Dev Bundella's family too improved its share both in *Zat* and *Sawar* mansab. Interestingly, Raja Jagat Singh's rebellion (1641-42) during this phase, seems to have no negative impact on the status of Raja Basu's family mansabwise. In fact its share in *Zat* and *Sawar* mansab seems to have doubled during this period.

Table 3-B contains statistics pertaining to the total awarded mansab during the three phases of Shah Jahan's reign, share of the Rajputs as a racial group, total mansab of the Rajput families and the mansab of all family groups.

This table shows that although the Rajput family groups formed the second largest faction after the Iranis, but among the family groups mansabwise their share was less than the Iranis. It was 20 per cent of the *Zat* and 19 per cent of *Sawar* mansab, held by the family groups collectively during the first phase. In the subsequent phases also, their proportion remains more or less the same.

These figures suggest another interesting feature. During the first phase these Rajput families shared about 72 per cent of the total *Zat* and 84 per cent of the total *Sawar* mansab held by their racial group. Their position further improved in the second phase as their share in the total mansab held by their racial group, reached 86 per cent in both the *Zat* and *Sawar*. In the last phase too their position was very strong vis-à-vis their own racial group mansabwise. So it may be said that the share of Rajput in total awarded mansab was basically a family-based award as was the case with the Iranis. Moreover, the larger share of some families in *Sawar* mansab than in *Zat* mansab, suggests that Shah Jahan was perhaps trying to keep the bulk of the *Sawars* under some trusted families. But while extending this favour he had to take extra precautions because these were the families of the zamindars who had a strong base in land too. That is why the families of only such trusted and confidant Rajput mansabdars like Gaj Singh, Jai Singh and Gopal Das Gaur held a larger share in the *Sawar* mansab and that too in the last phase.

Afghan Families

During the Mughal period, Afghans as a racial group rose to eminence only under Jahangir. Khan-i-Jahan Lodhi came so close to the emperor that he had no rivals at the court. Shah Jahan inaugurated his reign with a normal favourable policy towards this faction. Twenty-one Afghan nobles were promoted between February 1628 and April 1628.[18] Starting from a share of 11 per cent in the total strength of the nobility in the first phase, they gradually declined to 9 per cent in the second phase and to 8 per cent in the last phase.[19] Undoubtedly Kahn-i-Jahan Lodhi's rebellion had a negative impact on the fortunes of this group but they were not thrown out of favour completely. They still occupied an important position among the Indian nobles after the Rajputs and the Shaikhzadas.

Nine leading families of Afghan mansabdars, included

in this study, are enlisted along with their mansab in Table 4-A.

On the basis of the figures in Table 4-A, it may be said that in the first phase the two prominent families were those of Khan-i-Jahan Lodhi and Darya Khan Rohila. But Lodhi's rebellion and Rohila's active support to him had an adverse impact on the fortunes of these families. Lodhi's family disappears in the second and the third phase as none of its members could rise to the level of *Hazari*. Such an impact on Rohila's family is evident from the heavy curtailment in its mansab during the second phase. In the third phase, however, this family could again rise to eminence perhaps because of the valuable services rendered by his son Bahadur Khan Rohila. Its mansab both in *Zat* and *Sawar* was the highest among the Afghan families.

This table puts forward some such Afghan families which improved their mansab throughout this reign such as those of Rashid Khan, Muhammad Khan Niyaz, Mubariz Khan Rohila, Nazr Bahadur Kheshgi and Sher Khan Tarin, perhaps because of their unqualified support till the end of the Deccan campaigns.[20] Only two out of nine, namely the family of Khan-i-Jahan Lodhi and the family of Sher Khan Taunur, could not rise to the level of 1,000 *Zat* during the second and third phase.

Table 4-B provides relevant details pertaining to the total mansab award, share of the Afghans as a racial group, total mansab of the Afghan families and the total mansab held by all the family groups, during the three phases of this reign: 1628-36; 1637-41; 1642-58.

On the basis of the given figures it may be said that the position of the Afghan families vis-à-vis other family groups was not as strong as that of the Iranis. However, vis-à-vis their racial group they were in a strong position. During the first phase they enjoyed about 56 per cent of the *Zat* and 65 per cent of the *Sawar* mansab, collectively held by their racial group. In the subsequent phase their share in the total mansab of their racial group, further increased. And almost the same trend continued during the last phase too. It may therefore be said that the share of the Afghans in the total awarded mansab was also a family-based award like the Iranis and the Rajputs. Besides this the larger share of the Afghan families in the total *Sawar* mansab, held by their racial group, throughout this reign, implies greater trust placed in them. Hence the rebellion staged by an individual, belonging to a particular family, did not jeopardize the credibility of the Afghan family groups as such.

Families of the Indian Muslims

Indian Muslims[21] better known as Shaikhzadas came into the limelight between 1560 and 1575 when Akbar took to reorganize his nobility.[22] Henceforth they gradually carved out a place of distinction in the Mughal nobility.

Under Shah Jahan also they enjoyed a respectable position numberwise as well as mansabwise. During the succession tussle they sympathized with Asaf Khan. Syed Hizabr Khan Barha, Daulat Khan Mai, Syed Ja'far and Syed Alam Barha were active supporters of prince Shah Jahan. Therefore, out of 176 mansabdars who were the recipients of royal favours, immediately after the coronation, 20 were Indian Muslims.[23] During 1628-36 out of 342 mansabdars, 32 were Indian Muslims. They improved their strength between 1637-41 and reached the number of 28 out of 255. In the last phase, registering further improvement, they numbered 59 out of the total strength of 448.

During the two initial phases, Indian Muslims delivered their best on the battlefield and served remarkably well in administrative positions. Syed Shujat Khan Barha, Syed Alawal, Murtaza Khan, Jan Nisar Khan, Khan-i-Jahan Syed Muzaffar Khan Barha, etc. rendered remarkable services in the Deccan wars.[24] Indian Muslims also proved their worth as administrators both at the central and provincial levels.[25] The third phase proved to be most fertile for this group. Not only because of their gains numberwise and mansabwise but because of their elevation in administrative offices. Sa′dullah Khan was the first Indian Muslim to be appointed as *Diwan-i-kul* in 1645. He continued in this office till his death in 1656. Earlier he held the office of *Mir-e-Saman*. After Moosvi Khan, an Irani, all the *sadrs* were selected only from this group. Their representation increased notably in prestigious provincial offices too. All this confirms a higher degree of confidence placed in this faction.

The enviable position of the Indian Muslims is also reflected from their share in the total mansab, awarded during this reign.[26]

Twelve leading families of Indian Muslims are chosen for this study and relevant information pertaining to their mansab is arranged in Table 5-A. The table shows that among the Indian Muslim families, Khan-i-Jahan Barha's family enjoyed a distinguished status. This family started from 5,000 *Zat*, 10,000 *Sawar* and finally reached the mansab of 12,000 *Zat*, 14,500 *Sawar* without any loss. Hence this family was favoured most. Next to this, the families of Akbar Quli Gakkhar, Syed Bayazid, Ikhlas Khan Shaikh Farid, Murtaza Khan Syed Nizam and Dindar Khan Abdul Wahid were the recipients of great favours. None of these suffered any setbacks throughout this reign.

This table also suggests that most of these families made notable progress in the third phase. In the second phase, they generally had to remain content with their mansabs of the first phase. It is worth noting here that with the exception of Syed Bayazid's family none suffered any loss in mansab during this phase. The families of Akbar Quli and Hizabr Khan in fact gained 300 and 200 *Sawar* respectively. This point becomes more meaningful if we bear the fact in mind that during the second phase a large number of family groups among the Iranis, Afghans, Rajputs and Marathas, had to suffer setbacks in mansab. Indian Muslims and the Turanis virtually seem to have been exempted from this extensive curtailment, and this obviously hints at special treatment extended to them.

Our Table 5-B contains the data pertaining to the total award of mansab, the share of the Indian Muslims as a racial group, total mansab held by the Indian Muslim families and the total mansab of all family groups during the three phases of Shah Jahan's reign. The position of Indian Muslim families among other family groups and vis-à-vis their own racial group may be explained with the help of this table.

Like the Afghans, the Indian Muslim families also enjoyed more or less the same proportion among the family groups, which they as a racial group, held in the total awarded mansab during all the three phases.

Vis-à-vis their racial group, the position of the Indian Muslim families was not so sound as was the case with the Irani, Afghan and Rajput families, as they held almost half the total of their racial group in both *Zat* and *Sawar* mansab during all the three phases. This would mean that the share of Indian Muslims in the total awarded mansab was not exclusively based on the share of their family groups.

Maratha Families

In the words of Athar Ali, 'ever since, Malik Amber used the Maratha chiefs and their followers (*Bargirs*) on a large scale, the Mughals had begun to realize the value of the Marathas in the Deccan wars'.[27] So Jahangir recruited and made good use of them. During Shah Jahan's period, state policy towards the Marathas was usually guided by the fluctuations in the political and military conditions of the Deccan. Any rise or decline in their utility had an immediate reflection on their strength in the nobility. That was why their number increased during 1628-36 as hectic military activities continued in the Deccan. After the treaty of 1636 which brought comparative peace in the region for a period of about twenty years, the number of the Marathas consistently declined. From the figure of 32 out of 342 in the first phase, they came down to a number of 19 out of 255 in the second phase and in the last phase they numbered only 16 out of a total of 448.[28] Accordingly their share in total awarded mansab gradually declined during the three phases of Shah Jahan's reign.[29] Moreover the share of the Marathas in total *Sawar* mansab was always less than their share in the *Zat* mansab[30] which means they were not taken as confident and dependable servants of the Mughal emperor. This attitude might have some basis in the dubious and uncertain role of the Marathas from the very beginning. That is why, perhaps, we cannot compare the Marathas with the Rajputs vis-à-vis the Mughal ruler.

Regarding the Maratha families, the available information is arranged in Table 6-A. From the mansab figures of these four families, the eminence of Jagdev Rao's family becomes evident during the first phase. In the subsequent phase it had to suffer a loss of about 17,000 in *Zat* and of 15,000 in *Sawar* mansab, which was the highest among these families. The families of Kheluji and Udaji, who proved their loyalty, improved their position during the last phase. A comparatively higher share of Kheluji's family in *Sawar* mansab during this phase, implies greater imperial confidence in this family.

Table 6-B incorporates the statistics dealing with the total awarded mansab over the three phases of Shah Jahan's reign, share of the Maratha racial group in the total award, total mansab held by the Maratha families and the total mansab occupied by all the family groups.

The figures in this table suggest that the position of Maratha families among other family groups weakens after the first phase. In the first phase their share in total *Zat* and *Sawar* mansab, held by all the family groups, was about 14 per cent and 12 per cent respectively which was higher than the Turani, Afghan and Indian Muslim families. Subsequent phases witnessed a major setback in their status among the family groups.

But in their own racial group, the position of Maratha families was quite strong. During the first phase these families occupied almost 57 per cent of the total *Zat* and 61 per cent of the total *Sawar* mansab, held by their racial group. Although there was a decline in their share in the second phase, in the third phase they again improved in both the ranks vis-à-vis their racial group and attained almost the same proportion, they had enjoyed in the first phase. On the whole it may be said that the Maratha family groups enjoyed more favours than the Marathas as a racial group.

This primitive survey of the family groups of Mughal

mansabdars, with all its limitations, leads to the following conclusion which is purely tentative in nature.

During 1628-36 when the number of the nobility and the figures of the total awarded mansab notably increased owing to the well known reasons, these family groups enjoyed a superior position over the individual mansabdars of various ethnic groups; because their share in the total awarded *Zat* and *Sawar* mansab was about 58 per cent and 67 per cent respectively.

The second phase (1637-41) was a period of comparative peace with very few military engagements. Shah Jahan, therefore tried to exercise a certain control on the rising number of the nobility causing heavy curtailment (roughly more than 20%) in the number of the nobles as well as the total awarded mansab. The family groups also could not escape and lost almost 20 per cent in *Zat* and 21 per cent in *Sawar* mansab from their share they held in the preceding phase. This means that their larger share in the total mansab award, for all its serious implications, was noted. But this policy of checks and balances could not be pushed further due to the arising situation during 1642-58 which led to a tremendous surge in the overall strength of the nobility. These developments had a favourable impact on the fortune of these family groups as their loss (of about 20%) in both *Zat* and *Sawar* during the preceding phase was compensated with an immense rise (of more than 50%) in their share in both the ranks in the total mansab award of the last phase.

Thus, starting from a share of about 58 per cent in the total awarded *Zat* and about 67 per cent of the total granted *Sawar* mansab, these family groups with a slight decline in the second phase, finally occupied about 73 per cent of the total granted *Zat* and about 81 per cent of the total granted *Sawar* mansab. Could it therefore be said at least tentatively, that the bulk of the mansab, awarded during this reign, was occupied by the family groups of the mansabdars? That more confidence was placed in them is evident from their larger share in the total award of the *Sawar* mansab than in the *Zat*. All this, possibly, elevated their status and position vis-à-vis the individual mansabdars of various ethnic groups and also qualified them for a greater share in the resources of the empire.

The rise of such family groups with huge mansab and immense resources at their disposal, was bound to result in the concentration of power in a few hands. This could adversely affect the element of interdependence between the king and the nobility, gradually increasing the king's dependence on the latter. Thus, Akbar's effort to maintain an equilibrium between the two seems to be at stake. The thirteenth century preserves an interesting precedent of this kind when Iltutmish granted unprecedented favours to a few Turkish nobles who swiftly acquired control over the three major centres of authority namely, the charge of the royal household, provincial governorships and strategic military commands and played a key role in sealing the fate of his family during 1236-66.

Therefore, it can be suggested hypothetically that the trend of concentration of power in a few pockets, which was unfavourable to the medieval polity, passed almost unnoticed during Shah Jahan's period. This should have made the nobles more confident of their status and power as is reflected from Yamin-ud-daulah Asaf Khan's behaviour. During the Deccan wars in 1631-32 when the Khan was assigned the supreme command of the three armies, in a convivial party addressing Azam Khan, he said that the state's business would not be complete without them.[31] This hints at a growing feeling among some powerful nobles that the king was becoming more dependent upon them.

Since the share in power was an inbuilt issue of contradiction between the king and the nobility, it could be enhanced at the expense of the other. The possibilities of minimization or maximization of power on either side, however, depended on the prevailing conditions, policies and plans of the emperor and also the availability of suitable opportunities to both the king and the nobility.

Shah Jahan's mistake of heaping eggs in one basket back fired at the end. His illness was grasped as a ripe opportunity by the powerful nobles to push further ahead in the arena of power while by others to seek entry into it. Thus the cohesion between the king and the nobility, as well as among the nobles which rested on the basic element of mutual interdepdence, was utterly destroyed. This is confirmed from the division of the nobles into two camps during 1658-59. The exhaustive list of Athar Ali suggests that out of 231 nobles who participated in this armed struggle, only 87 were on Shah Jahan's side while the majority, i.e. 144 joined the rebel princes. More interesting is the fact that the number of the most favoured Iranis enjoying a distinct and elevated status among all the family groups, was larger in the opposition camp. Only the Rajputs and the Indian Muslims in an overwhelming majority supported Shah Jahan, showing their satisfaction with the remarkable progress they had made during these thirty years. On the other hand the Afghans and the Marathas who were on the lowest pedestal, in order to jump to a higher level, sided with the younger princes in overwhelming numbers.

In the light of the above, it can it be suggested, purely on a temporary basis, that besides many other factors, the crisis of 1658-59, was also the result of Shah Jahan's inability to maintain a stable equilibrium between the elements of interdependence and contradiction, governing the basic relationship between the king and the nobility. Perhaps that was why Shah Jahan's depositioin and long confinement at Agra for about eight years, passed almost unnoticed as a matter of no concern, devoid of any significance; although this occurrence was the first of its nature in Mughal history.

After 1658, the war of succession became a pre-condition for accession to the Mughal throne. This accelerated the process of transfer of power in a few selected hands, which continued eclipsing the powers of the Mughal ruler proportionately. The days were not far ahead when the emperor was cast into a historic artifact to grace the showcase of Indian polity. His individual relevance was replaced with his institutional significance. The descendant of Akbar, 'The Great', was moulded into a celebrity to be adored only occasionally. The couplet attributed to Shah Alam II: *Subh to Jam se guzarti hai, Shabdil aram se guzarti hai, Aqibat ki khabar khuda jane, ab to aram se guzarti hai* may not be dismissed as mere imagery or verbosity of a poet, perhaps it echoes the agony of the ruined. The same anguish is imbibed in the following couplet of Bahadur Shah Zafar:

> *Mera rang roop bigar giya, mera yar mujhse bichar gaya,*
> *Jo chaman khazan se ujar gaya, mein usiki fasl-e-bahar hun.*

I close with the submission that the suggestions made over here, should be taken as purely tentative and conjectural in nature, which need to be qualified with more delicate research and able attention of the scholars of medieval India.

Table 1A: Mansab of Irani Families

	1628-36	*1637-41*	*1642-58*
	Yamin-ud-daulah Asaf Khan's family		
Zat	31,000	25,000	35,000
Sawar	36,100	33,400	31,300
	Rustam Khan Safavi's family		
Zat	15,000	13,000	21,500
Sawar	10,400	8,450	20,500
	Amir ul-Umara Ali Mardan Khan's family		
Zat	—	7,000	15,000
Sawar	—	10,000	15,900
	Islam Khan Mashhadi's family		
Zat	5,000	5,000	14,000
Sawar	10,000	8,000	14,600
	Azam Khan's family		
Zat	7,500	7,500	12,500
Sawar	6,500	6,600	10,500
	Khalilullah Khan's family		
Zat	6,000	5,000	14,500
Sawar	3,700	4,000	10,700
	Iftikhar Khan Turkman's family		
Zat	6,500	8,000	11,000
Sawar	4,800	6,750	9,500
	Illuhwardi Khan's family		
Zat	7,000	8,000	8,500
Sawar	6,000	7,000	6,000
	Mahabat Khan's family		
Zat	14,000	7,000	5,000
Sawar	24,000	11,000	3,000

	Saif Khan Mirza Safi's family		
Zat	6,000	6,000	5,500
Sawar	4,600	4,600	1,450
	Zain Khan Koka's family		
Zat	4,500	4,000	8,000
Sawar	3,200	3,000	6,800
	Khwaja Abul Hasan's family		
Zat	9,000	3,000	5,500
Sawar	8,000	2,000	2,200
	Qasim Khan Namkin's family		
Zat	4,000	4,000	5,500
Sawar	2,200	2,300	3,100
	Baqar Khan Najm-i-Sani's family		
Zat	6,000	7,000	2,500
Sawar	5,500	5,700	1,000
	Lashkar Khan Abul Hasan Mashhadi's family		
Zat	8,500	4,000	4,000
Sawar	7,800	3,500	1,700
	Mirza Khan Manochahar's family		
Zat	4,000	3,000	4,000
Sawar	2,500	2,000	3,250
	Asaf Khan Jafar Beg's family		
Zat	4,000	1,500	2,500
Sawar	3,100	1,500	1,500
	Afzal Khan Allami's family		
Zat	7,000	9,500	4,000
Sawar	4,100	4,600	3,000
	Safshikan Khan Mirza Lashkari's family		
Zat	6,000	2,500	3,500
Sawar	3,800	2,000	2,600
	Jansipar Khan Turkman's family		
Zat	6,000	1,000	
Sawar	7,600	600	—

	Hakim Hammam's family		
Zat	3,000	1,000	1,000
Sawar	500	200	200
	Qazalbash Khan Afshar's family		
Zat	2,000	3,000	6,000
Sawar	1,000	3,000	6,000
	Zulfiqar Khan Khanlar's family		
Zat	1,500	1,500	5,000
Sawar	800	800	6,800
	Zabardast Khan's family		
Zat	1,500	1,500	4,500
Sawar	1,000	1,000	2,500

Table 1B: Share of Irani Racial Group and Irani Family Groups in Total Awarded Mansab

	Total awarded mansab	*Share of Irani racial group*	*Total mansab of Irani family groups*	*Total mansab of all family groups*
		1628-36		
Zat	7,44,000	2,48,000	1,65,000	4,34,000
Sawar	5,93,322	2,08,122	1,57,200	3,94,600
		1637-41		
Zat	5,45,500	1,97,500	1,38,000	3,25,500
Sawar	4,54,950	1,68,900	1,32,000	3,09,850
		1642-58		
Zat	8,98,500	3,00,500	1,98,500	5,46,500
Sawar	7,22,000	2,32,550	1,64,100	4,81,550

Table 2A: Mansab of Turani Families

	1628-36	*1637-41*	*1642-58*
Abdullah Khan Firoz Jang's family			
Zat	11,500	12,000	18,500
Sawar	8,600	9,000	18,300
Said Khan Zafar Jang's family			
Zat	11,500	10,000	19,500
Sawar	12,300	14,400	21,100
Isa Tarkhan's family			
Zat	5,000	6,000	9,000
Sawar	10,000	6,500	13,500
Khan-i-Dauran Nusrat Jang's family			
Zat	5,000	6,000	11,500
Sawar	10,000	12,000	14,900
Najabat Khan Mirza Shuja's family			
Zat	3,000	4,000	7,500
Sawar	2,000	4,000	5,200
Qulij Khan's family			
Zat	4,000	6,000	8,500
Sawar	5,000	7,500	11,500
Uzbek Khan Nazar Bahadur Kheshgi's family			
Zat	1,000	2,000	4,500
Sawar	1,000	1,400	4,000
Khusrau's (S/o Nazar Muhammad Khan) family			
Zat	—	—	17,500
Sawar	—	—	6,100

Table 2B: Share of Turani Racial Group and Turani Family Groups in Total Awarded Mansab

	Total awarded mansab	*Share of Irani racial group*	*Total mansab of Irani family groups*	*Total mansab of all family groups*
		1628-36		
Zat	7,44,000	1,22,000	41,000	4,34,000
Sawar	5,93,322	1,01,100	43,000	3,94,600
		1637-41		
Zat	5,45,500	1,21,000	46,000	3,25,500
Sawar	4,54,950	1,09,700	54,800	3,09,850
		1642-58		
Zat	8,98,500	2,19,000	96,500	5,46,500
Sawar	7,22,000	1,76,100	94,600	4,81,550

Table 3A: Mansab of Rajput Families

	1628-36	*1637-41*	*1642-58*
	Raja Gaj Singh's family		
Zat	13,000	16,500	23,500
Sawar	9,300	15,500	21,500
	Rao Sur Bhurtiya's family		
Zat	6,000	3,000	8,000
Sawar	4,500	2,100	6,500
	Raja Jai Singh's Family		
Zat	10,500	6,000	10,000
Sawar	6,500	5,700	12,900
	Rao Ratan Hara's family		
Zat	12,000	6,000	10,000
Sawar	10,200	5,500	9,000
	Bir Narain Badgujar's family		
Zat	4,000	4,000	2,000
Sawar	2,100	2,500	1,500

	Kishan Singh Bhadoriya's family		
Zat	1,000	1,000	3,500
Sawar	600	600	2,800
	Bir Singh Dev Bundela's family		
Zat	22,000	8,000	10,500
Sawar	17,800	5,400	9,900
	Rai Sal Darbari's family		
Zat	3,500	1,000	1,000
Sawar	2,200	500	500
	Pirthi Raj Rathor's family		
Zat	2,000	2,000	3,000
Sawar	1,000	1,700	2,500
	Rao Chanda's family		
Zat	3,500	1,500	5,500
Sawar	2,500	1,000	3,200
	Gopal Das Gaur's family		
Zat	4,500	6,500	15,000
Sawar	3,000	5,000	18,900
	Raja Basu's family		
Zat	3,000	3,000	6,000
Sawar	500	2,000	4,500
	Rana Karan's family		
Zat	13,000	8,000	24,000
Sawar	11,500	7,000	15,500
	Rawal Ponja's family		
Zat	1,000	1,500	2,500
Sawar	500	1,500	2,500
	Ramdas Narauri's family		
Zat	2,000	3,000	1,500
Sawar	1,000	1,600	1,000

Table 3B: Share of Rajput Racial Group and Rajput Family Groups in Total Awarded Mansab

	Total awarded mansab	*Share of Rajput racial group*	*Total mansab of Rajput family groups*	*Total mansab of all family groups*
		1628-36		
Zat	7,44,000	1,21,500	88,000	4,34,000
Sawar	5,93,322	86,900	73,200	3,94,600
		1637-41		
Zat	5,45,500	82,500	71,000	3,25,500
Sawar	4,54,950	66,400	57,600	3,09,850
		1642-58		
Zat	8,98,500	1,53,500	1,26,000	5,46,500
Sawar	7,22,000	1,31,500	1,12,700	4,81,550

Table 4A: Mansab of Afghan Families

	1628-36	*1637-41*	*1642-58*
	Rashid Khan Ansari's family		
Zat	4,000	5,000	9,500
Sawar	3,600	5,000	9,500
	Sahbaz Khan Rohila's family		
Zat	5,000	2,500	2,500
Sawar	3,400	2,000	2,000
	Muhammad Khan Niyazi's family		
Zat	4,500	4,500	5,000
Sawar	4,000	4,000	5,000
	Khan-i-Jahan Lodhi's family		
Zat	9,000	—	—
Sawar	14,900	—	—
	Darya Khan Rohila's family		
Zat	9,000	5,000	13,000
Sawar	8,700	7,700	16,300

	Mubariz Khan Rohila's family		
Zat	3,500	4,000	5,000
Sawar	3,500	4,000	4,600
	Nazr Bahadur Kheshgi's family		
Zat	2,000	3,500	8,500
Sawar	1,500	2,300	8,900
	Sher Khan Taunur's family		
Zat	6,500	—	—
Sawar	6,000	—	—
	Sher Khan Tarin's family (zamindar)		
Zat	2,000	2,000	3,000
Sawar	1,000	1,000	1,600

Table 4B: Share of Afghan Racial Group and Afghan Family Groups in Total Awarded Mansab

	Total awarded mansab	*Share of Afghan racial group*	*Total mansab of Afghan family groups*	*Total mansab of all family groups*
		1628-36		
Zat	7,44,000	80,500	45,500	4,34,000
Sawar	5,93,322	70,950	46,600	3,94,600
		1637-41		
Zat	5,45,500	44,000	26,500	3,25,500
Sawar	4,54,950	33,300	26,000	3,09,850
		1642-58		
Zat	8,98,500	75,000	46,500	5,46,500
Sawar	7,22,000	69,000	47,900	4,81,550

Table 5A: Mansab of Indian Muslim Families

	1628-36	*1637-41*	*1642-58*
	Akbar Quli Gakkhar's family		
Zat	1,500	1,500	4,000
Sawar	1,200	1,500	3,400

	Hizabr Khan Barha's family		
Zat	5,000	5,000	3,000
Sawar	1,800	2,000	1,800
	Syed Bayazid's family		
Zat	6,000	4,000	10,000
Sawar	2,700	8,000	11,300
	Syed Diler Khan Barha's family		
Zat	4,000	—	3,000
Sawar	3,000	—	3,000
	Syed Yaqub Bukhari's family		
Zat	2,500	—	—
Sawar	1,700	—	—
	Ikhlas Khan Shaikh Farid's family		
Zat	5,500	5,500	9,000
Sawar	3,300	3,300	6,300
	Syed Khan-i-Jahan Barha's family		
Zat	5,000	5,000	12,000
Sawar	10,000	10,000	14,500
	Murtaza Khan Syed Nizam's family		
Zat	3,000	3,000	4,000
Sawar	2,000	2,000	2,700
	Mahmud Khan's family		
Zat	3,000	—	1,000
Sawar	1,000		1000
	Dindar Khan Abdul Wahid's family		
Zat	—	1,000	2,000
Sawar		650	1,650
	Syed Muhammad S/o Syed Afzal's family		
Zat	—	—	2,000
Sawar	—	—	1,100
	Syed Jalal Bukhari S/o Syed Muhammad Bukhari's family		
Zat	—	—	8,500
Sawar	—	—	2,500

Table 5B: Share of Indian Muslim Racial Group and Indian Muslim Family Groups in Total Awarded Mansab

	Total awarded mansab	*Share of Indian Muslim racial group*	*Total mansab of Indian Muslim family groups*	*Total mansab of all family groups*
		1628-36		
Zat	7,44,000	68,500	35,500	4,34,000
Sawar	5,93,322	48,700	26,700	3,94,600
		1637-41		
Zat	5,45,500	58,000	25,000	3,25,500
Sawar	4,54,950	51,950	27,450	3,09,850
		1642-58		
Zat	8,98,500	1,14,000	58,500	5,46,500
Sawar	7,22,000	92,450	49,250	4,81,550

Table 6A: Manasab of Maratha Families

	1628-36	*1637-41*	*1642-58*
	Jagdev Rao's family		
Zat	25,000	8,000	9,500
Sawar	18,500	3,500	4,000
	Kheluji's family		
Zat	13,000	8,000	8,000
Sawar	11,500	6,500	7,000
	Udaji's family		
Zat	11,000	3,000	3,000
Sawar	9,000	2,000	2,000
	Sahuji's family		
Zat	10,000	—	—
Sawar	8,000	—	—

Table 6B: Share of Maratha Racial Group and Maratha Family Groups in Total Awarded Mansab

	Total awarded mansab	*Share of Maratha racial group*	*Total mansab of Maratha family groups*	*Total mansab of all family groups*
		1628-36		
Zat	7,44,000	1,03,500	59,000	4,34,000
Sawar	5,93,322	77,550	47,000	3,94,600
		1637-41		
Zat	5,45,500	42,500	19,000	3,25,500
Sawar	4,54,950	24,700	12,000	3,09850
		1642-58		
Zat	8,98,500	36,500	20,500	5,46,500
Sawar	7,22,000	20,400	13,000	4,81,550

Note: The total awarded mansab does not include the share of 'other Muslims' and 'other Hindus'.

NOTES

1. For a detailed discussion on this theme see S. Nurul Hasan, 'New Light on the Relations of the Early Mughal Rulers with Their Nobility', I.H.C., 1944.
2. See S.A.A. Rizvi, *Religious and Intellectual History of the Muslims in Akbar's Reign*, Delhi, 1975, Chapter 10; also I.A. Khan, 'Nobility under Akbar and the Development of His Religious Policy', *J.R.A.S.*, London, 1968.
3. Lahori, I, pp. 254-5, 395, 495-6; Lahori, II, pp. 269-70, 276-8, 285, 291; M.U., II, pp. 420, 448.
4. M.U. II, p. 733
5. Ibid., p. 448; Salih, III, p. 217.
6. Appendix 2. Also Firdos Anwar, *Nobility under the Mughals (1628-58)*, Delhi, 2001, Chapter 2.
7. Ibid.
8. Ibid.
9. For example, Afzal Husain's, *Nobility under Akbar and Jahangir*

– *A Study of Family Groups*, Delhi, 1999.

10. For their numerical strength and their share in mansab see Firdos Anwar, *Nobility under the Mughals (1628-58)*, Delhi, pp. 29-30 and 79. Also Appendices 1 and 3 in this paper.
11. Lahori, pp. 70-71.
12. Ibid.
13. Ibid., pp. 72-3.
14. Ibid., pp. 113, 117-23, 158-61, 176-7, 180-6, 195, 202-3.
15. See Appendix 1, 2 and 3.
16. Z. Kh., I, p. 104.
17. Lahori, I, pp. 113, 117-23, 158-61, 176-7, 180-6 and 202-3.
18. Lahori, I, pp. 113, 117-23, 158-61, 176-7, 180-6, 195 and 202-3.
19. Firdos Anwar, op. cit., p. 32. Also Appendix 1 of this paper.
20. Lahori, I, pp. 298, 300-1, 356-61, 496-9, 500-1, 508-11, 512-9, 521, 525, 537-8; I (b) pp. 35-40, 43-4, 46, 135-6, 140, 177, 217-8, 220-1 and 225.
21. Manucci, II, pp. 426-7. Also Iqtidar Alam Khan, 'The Nobility under Akbar and the Development of His Religious Policy', *J.R.A.S.*, London 1968.
22. Ibid.
23. Lahori, I, pp. 113, 117-23, 158-61, 176-7, 180-6, 195 and 202-3.
24. See Firdos Anwar, op. cit., pp. 54, 58, 68 etc.
25. Ibid.
26. See Table 5-B.
27. Athar Ali, *The Mughal Nobility under Aurangzeb,* Bombay, 1968, p. 29.
28. Firdos Anwar, op. cit., pp. 35-6.
29. Ibid., Chapter IV.
30. Ibid. Also Appendix 3 of this paper.
31. M.U., I, p. 157.

Appendix 1: Numerical Strength of the Racial and Religious Groups (During the Three Phases)

Mansab	*Iranis*	*Turanis*	*Afghans*	*Indian Muslims*	*Other Muslims*	*Rajputs*	*Marathas*	*Other Hindus*	*Grand Total*
				1626-36					
5000 Zat and above	14	6	2	2	2	6	6	–	38
3000 to 4500 Zat	21	12	9	6	10	12	9	–	79
1000 to 2700 Zat	58	35	26	24	27	35	17	3	225
Grand total	**93**	**53**	**37**	**32**	**39**	**53**	**32**	**3**	**342**
				1637-41					
5000 Zat and above	12	7	1	2	–	4	1	–	27
3000 to 4500 Zat	18	10	2	5	5	8	6	–	54
1000 to 2700 Zat	45	33	21	21	11	29	12	2	174
Grand total	**75**	**50**	**24**	**28**	**16**	**41**	**19**	**2**	**255**
				1642-58					
5000 Zat and above	15	10	1	5	–	6	1	–	38
3000 to 4500 Zat	23	17	8	5	7	15	6	–	81
1000 to 2700 Zat	94	69	29	49	19	53	9	7	329
Grand Total	**132**	**96**	**38**	**59**	**26**	**74**	**16**	**7**	**448**

Note: Other Muslims and other Hindus are not included in this study.

Appendix 2: Number of Khanazads Among the Mansabdars of Shah Jahan

Mansab	*Total*	*Khanazads*
	1628-36	
5000 *Zat* and above	38	23
3000 *Zat* to 4500	79	45
1000 to 2700 *Zat*	225	93
Grand Total	**342**	**161**
	1637-41	
5000 *Zat* and above	27	19
3000 to 4500 *Zat*	54	32
1000 to 2700 *Zat*	174	78
Grand Total	**255**	**129**
	1642-58	
5000 *Zat* and above	38	25
3000 to 4500 *Zat*	81	51
1000 to 2700 *Zat*	329	175
Grand Total	**448**	**251**

Appendix 3: Total Grant of *Zat* and *Sawar* Mansab (During the Three Phases)

	Iranis	*Turanis*	*Afghans*	*Indian Muslims*	*Rajputs*	*Marathas*	*Grand Total*
				1628-36			
Zat	2,48,000	1,22,000	80,500	68,500	1,21,500	1,03,500	7,44,000
Sawar	2,08,122	1,01,100	70,950	48,700	86,900	77,550	5,93,322
				1637-41			
Zat	1,97,500	1,21,000	44,000	58,000	82,500	42,500	5,45,500
Sawar	1,68,900	1,09,700	33,300	51,950	66,400	24,700	4,54,950
				1642-58			
Zat	3,00,500	2,19,000	75,000	1,14,000	1,53,500	36,500	8,98,500
Sawar	2,32,550	1,76,100	69,000	92,450	1,31,500	20,400	7,22,000